TABLE OF CONTENTS

BEFORE YOU BEGIN:

WHO THIS IS FOR AND WHAT YOU'LL LEARN

Throughout this book, I will use the word instructor. But don't let that limit you. If you are responsible for helping others improve—whether that's children, teens, or adults—this book is for you. At its core, this book holds one major lesson, and that lesson is how to encourage excellence instead of coercing compliance or bribing cooperation.

By the end, you'll be able to cultivate respect without fear or showmanship, transfer skills through an effective, proven six-step process, and create students who push themselves even when you're not watching.

You might see yourself as a teacher in a classroom, a coach on the field, a mentor in business, or a leader in your community. The principles inside these pages apply wherever people are learning, growing, and being guided.

I've seen the MENTOR Method work in every setting imaginable, including the most personal one: my home. My wife and I are raising a 12-year-old son who is autistic and nonverbal. Every single day, we use the principles in this book with him. We measure where he is, establish clear expectations, notice his progress, test his understanding, observe his growth, and remind him when needed. This method isn't just a theory that I teach at the studio. It's how we communicate, connect, and help our son grow. If these principles can work in one of the most challenging teaching environments there is, they can work wherever you are.

ABOUT THE AUTHOR

Bronson Ko is the founder and CEO of Ko Martial Arts (KOMA), a premier martial arts organization based in the Kansas City area that has become a respected model for modern martial arts education—known for its structure, discipline, and mentorship-driven culture.

Above all, Bronson's greatest priority is to serve God in everything he does. His purpose in business and teaching is to glorify Christ by helping others grow in character, confidence, and resilience. Every part of KOMA—from its curriculum to its leadership development—is built on faith, integrity, and excellence.

With more than 25 years of teaching experience, Bronson developed The MENTOR Method, a framework that helps instructors connect with students of all ages through calm authority, clear structure, and genuine care. His approach blends biblical principles, traditional martial arts values, and modern developmental insight—creating students who are strong in both skill and spirit.

Bronson has been married to his better half for 16 years, and together they are blessed with a 12-year-old son who is autistic and nonverbal, and a daughter. Not only has Bronson taught countless students on the autism spectrum over the years, but he and his wife use the MENTOR Method with their son every day, breaking down expectations, celebrating small wins, and building communication one step at a time. His greatest joy comes from leading his family in faith and purpose while building a legacy that honors God.

Today, he continues to lead the expansion of the KOMA Franchise, training and equipping school owners across the country to impact their communities through faith-based mentorship and world-class instruction. His mission is to glorify God by building a network of leaders who teach with excellence, lead with humility, and help others become who they were created to be.

To my Lord and Savior, Jesus Christ—May every word in this book bring glory to You.

To my better half, whose love, wisdom, and support have strengthened me through every season, and to our beautiful twins, who remind me daily why teaching with patience and purpose matters most.

This book is especially for instructors who:

- Want their students to not only learn skills, but also grow as people.

- Feel the weight of leading groups and wonder how to keep attention, focus, and respect.

- Have struggled with burnout and want tools that make teaching sustainable.

- Desire to move past old methods of yelling, intimidation, or "tippy-toe" avoidance and instead use a framework that balances connection and accountability.

- Care about leaving a lasting impact on the students they serve.

This is not just a book about teaching skills. It's about shaping lives. It's about becoming the kind of instructor your students will remember years later—the one who helped them grow stronger, more focused, and more resilient than they ever thought possible.

PART 1:

THREE METHODS, ONE CHOICE

Methods matter. The way you lead shapes not just today's class, but who your students become six months from now. In the pages ahead, we'll look at three common approaches you'll see in gyms, classrooms, and studios: the **Authoritative Method**, the **Tippy Toe Method**, and the **MENTOR Method**.

As you read each one, watch for three things:

- **What drives effort** (fear, being liked, or respect and ownership).
- **What happens when you're not there** (does the effort disappear or persist)?
- **What kind of student does it produce** over time (compliant, comfortable, or committed)?

This isn't about judging the past or shaming anyone. It's about clarity. See the strengths. See the limits. Then choose the path that creates durable growth. We'll start with **The Authoritative Method**.

THE AUTHORITATIVE METHOD

I started martial arts when I was three years old. My dad is a first-generation grandmaster from South Korea. He fought in the Vietnam War as part of the South Korean military, as an ally to America. You can probably guess how he raised me: very strict, very structured, no hugs or soft feelings, and a "my way or the highway" mindset.

Back then, not many kids did martial arts. Most students were adults. The way we were taught felt like the military. There was not much talking, just a lot of yelling and giving orders. The rule was simple: do what I say or face the consequences. Why did we try so hard? Was it because we wanted to improve? A little. But most of it was fear. We were afraid of getting in trouble. That could mean getting yelled at in front of everyone or doing knuckle pushups in the up position. I still remember the puddle of tears I left on the thin carpet we trained on. We did not have soft mats back then.

I call this the **Authoritative Method**.

To be clear, my dad developed a lot of strong students. They had great technique and mental toughness. Many of them went on to open their own martial arts schools. I still use many lessons I learned from him today. Overall, he was a great instructor who cared for his students. But that was a different time. Kids today live in a very different world.

The main reason I do not use the Authoritative Method today is simple: it is not the most effective. Especially not with today's kids. And it is not just about the kids. It is also about the parents.

For example, I wanted to quit martial arts many times as a kid. But I did not quit, because my dad did not let me. Most parents today let their kids quit the moment they complain. How do I know? I have seen it happen over and over again in the past twenty years of running Ko Martial Arts. We now have several locations, and this problem has only gotten worse over the last five years.

If we used the old method in our classes today, we would lose students fast. A child would feel bored or uncomfortable, tell their parents, and the parent would pull them out. When I was a kid, my parents usually sided with the teacher or coach. Today, parents are more likely to side with their child and blame the teacher. I do not agree with this way of doing things, but it is the world we live in. I could either complain about it or adapt. I choose the latter.

Now, let's go back to why the Authoritative Method does not work well today. The biggest problem is that it only works for a short time. It depends on fear. The instructor is the one pushing the student to try hard. But when the instructor is not around, the student stops trying. This method can still teach skills, but it usually takes longer and creates problems for some kids. Sensitive kids often shut down when pushed too hard. It seems there are many more sensitive kids today than before.

I care more about a method that works well and helps students grow for the long term. That is why I created the MENTOR Method. The biggest difference between the MENTOR Method and the old ways is this: it does not depend on outside pressure.

The Authoritative Method relies on fear as the primary motivator. Students try hard to avoid consequences such as push-ups, yelling, or embarrassment. But once the threat disappears, so does the effort.

It seems like many parents who were raised with the strict method have gone the other way. They do not want their children to feel the same struggle and discomfort they felt. They want their children to like them. They want their children to have a comfortable life. And that brings us to one of the most common teaching styles today: the Tippy Toe Method.

THE TIPPY TOE METHOD

I remember when the self-esteem movement was at its peak. In the 80s and 90s, schools and parents were told that self-esteem was the key to success. If kids just felt good about themselves, they would do better. Out of this came new programs, parenting styles, and coaching methods.

This way of thinking eventually reached martial arts and sports. Instructors, teachers, and parents started to believe that the best way to guide children was to avoid making them feel bad. Instead of being direct, adults began to tiptoe around behavior, never calling it out, and always trying to keep kids happy.

I call this the **Tippy Toe Method**.

The idea behind this method is simple: if you keep a child busy, happy, and distracted, they won't have time to misbehave. Instead of confronting bad behavior, the adult just focuses on rewarding good behavior. On the surface, it looks positive. Classes are high-energy, full of smiles, and fast-paced. But underneath, it leaves big gaps.

Here's the contrast: the Authoritative Method was all about fear and confrontation. The Tippy Toe Method avoids confrontation altogether. Both are extreme approaches. The Authoritative approach tells kids, "Do this or else." The Tippy Toe approach tells kids, "As long as you're smiling, we're good." Neither works long-term.

The biggest weakness of the Tippy Toe Method is the lack of feedback. Children need to know when they are right and when they are wrong. In my opinion, there is no such thing as good or bad feedback—there is only feedback. Without correction, kids will repeat the same mistakes until life—or another person—finally teaches them the hard way. That's why the "everyone gets a trophy" idea fails. It removes the chance to face failure, learn from it, and grow stronger. It is only when we fail that we know what *not* to do. Failure acts as the compass of what works and what doesn't.

Many adults also use the Tippy Toe Method because they want to be liked. Parents fear that correcting their child will make them look mean. Coaches avoid confrontation because they want to be the "fun" coach. Teachers think students will tune them out if they are too firm. But here's the truth: kids actually respect adults more when they set boundaries and give clear feedback. They may not say it at the moment, but over time, they feel safer and more cared for with structure.

Here's another idea to consider. Who cares if a child likes you or not! Their feelings can change at any moment. If you truly care about a child, you would put their well-being and long-term future ahead of whether they like you or not.

The first step is simple: stop baby talking to kids. Baby voices create confusion. They may make the adult feel softer, but they do not help the child understand. Children are not babies. They are intelligent human beings who deserve clear, direct, and respectful communication. Baby talk belongs with babies—and maybe with your dog when you come home from work, not in a classroom or on the practice field.

The Tippy Toe Method is built on fear, too. The fear of not being liked. The fear of having to deal with inappropriate behavior. But real respect does not come from tiptoeing around behavior. It comes from treating kids as capable people who deserve both encouragement *and* correction.

And that brings us to the MENTOR Method, which builds on the strengths of both approaches while avoiding their weaknesses.

THE MENTOR METHOD

The Authoritative and Tippy Toe approaches can both produce some positive results. But in my opinion, there is a more effective way—a method I call the MENTOR Method.

This method comes from my years of teaching children since I was 15. It grew through many trials and errors, failed lessons, and moments where sweat dripped down my back because I didn't know what to do with a child who was ignoring everything I asked him to do. And to make it worse, the parent was watching closely, waiting for my next move as their four-year-old challenged my authority.

The MENTOR Method is about using your voice to guide the child to *choose* to follow your request. The word that matters here is *choose*. Why is this important? Because a person gives their best effort only when they decide to act on their own. That is what I am most interested in. God made everyone unique, with different strengths, weaknesses, and desires. Every person is capable of giving their best effort. Personal excellence only happens when a student gives their full effort. Guiding them to that level should be a top priority for every instructor.

The MENTOR Method does not use fear to motivate. It does not depend on over-the-top energy or fake excitement. It is about human connection and meaningful conversations with the goal of building intrinsic motivation. This means guiding the child to make the right decision for themselves. While the Authoritative approach places the instructor in the role of dictator, and the Tippy Toe approach places the instructor in the role of entertainer, the MENTOR Method positions the instructor as a guide. A guide the student feels connected to, and most importantly, respects.

Let me show you what this looks like in practice. Imagine a four-year-old student who won't sit still during class.

The Authoritative instructor would bark: 'Sit down now or you're doing pushups!' The child complies out of fear, but the moment the instructor looks away, they're wiggling again. Fear only works when the threat is present.

The Tippy Toe instructor would try to distract them: 'Oh look, everyone! Let's play a fun game! Come on, let's all sit down together!' The child might sit briefly, but they've learned that misbehavior leads to entertainment. The instructor becomes a performer, not a leader.

The MENTOR instructor takes a different path. They kneel down, make eye contact, and ask calmly: 'What should you be doing right now?' The child thinks for a moment, then says quietly, 'Sitting.' The instructor nods: 'That's right. Can you show me how you sit in class?' The child sits properly. 'Perfect. That's exactly what I needed to see. Thank you.'

Notice what happened. The child chose to sit. They answered their own question. They felt respected, not controlled. And most importantly, they're learning to monitor their own behavior instead of waiting for the instructor to catch them.

LIKED VS. RESPECTED

What is the difference between being liked and respected?

Being liked is about how a person makes you feel when you are around them. Someone can be liked within seconds of meeting. Maybe they make you laugh or feel good about yourself. But those feelings can fade quickly when the person leaves. They can also change just as quickly because liking someone is based on emotions. Liking a person is often about entertainment. You want to be around them because they are fun, not boring, and easy to get along with.

Being respected is different. Respect is about what you think of a person as a whole—their qualities, principles, work ethic, integrity, and character. Respect takes time. Only by watching someone's behavior over time can you see who they really are, especially when it comes to work ethic. Many people can work hard for a day. Few can work hard for months or years. Respect is earned by doing the hard things most people avoid but wish they could do. It is not about being entertaining. It is about walking the hard road—the road people want to follow but need a guide to show them the way.

The MENTOR Method focuses on earning respect first and being liked second. It is about leading by example and showing students they are in good hands. The instructor shows what respect and humility look like by treating students with respect and humility.

Feedback is given regularly, reflecting the instructor's commitment to ensuring the student truly learns. Success is only reached when the student can perform the skill or explain the knowledge on their own, without the instructor's help.

RESPECT MISUNDERSTOOD

Some people think that if an instructor focuses on respect first, it makes them bossy or mean instead of kind. This is a misunderstanding. Many believe respect is earned by showing dominance, acting like a drill sergeant, barking orders, and belittling anyone who falls short. This can create fear, but fear does not build inner drive.

The MENTOR Method earns respect differently. It starts with connection. The instructor builds rapport and learns about the student—what they like, what they struggle with, and their unique personality. The interesting part is that this often makes the student like the instructor as well. But here's the difference: in the MENTOR Method, the instructor does not care about being liked. In the Tippy Toe approach, the instructor cares a lot about being liked. Students feel the difference. And people, including kids, prefer being around someone who does not obsess over being liked. They care more about how they are treated and whether the other person truly cares about them.

Now that we have touched on the MENTOR Method, let's move to the next step: understanding the importance of first leading yourself before leading others.

PART 2

LEADER, LEAD THYSELF

THE IMPORTANCE OF PRESENCE

0% of what kids hear from you isn't your words. It's how you say it and how you carry yourself."

– Dr. Albert Mehrabian, nonverbal communication expert

The way you express your thoughts can matter as much as the thoughts themselves. Before we dive deeper into the MENTOR Method, we need to talk about presence.

Presence is the feeling you give others the moment you walk into a room. It's the first impression people get, and it happens fast. Based on this feeling, people quickly decide whether or not they want to listen to you. The human eye can notice details of your presence in less than a second. In that instant, people pick up on:

- Posture
- Eye contact
- Facial expression
- Speed of movement
- Energy level

By the time you stand in front of your students, they've already judged you—without even realizing it. Before you say a single word, your presence has spoken for you. The real question is: what can you do to make sure your students see you as a leader worth following?

Here's why your presence is so critical: Students can only do their best if they can trust and respect the person leading them. Fear-based authority could compel them to follow you, but it can't ignite the passion to develop mastery. Entertainment-based energy could excite them at first glance, but it won't ignite their passion. When your presence exudes calmness, confidence, and commitment, your students will feel comfortable and inspired enough to stop performing for you and begin challenging themselves.

The goal is to carry a presence that shows three traits, all starting with the letter C: calm, confident, and committed.

Calm

Why calm? Doesn't that make kids think they can walk all over you? That's a common thought, but it's wrong. Many adults believe they need to be full of energy and excitement when teaching kids. The problem is that this often communicates the opposite of strength. Students want to follow leaders who are calm and steady, especially when things go wrong. Calm shows you can make the right choices under pressure. If you come across as anxious or stressed, you're telling your students you can't handle leading them.

But don't confuse calm with being lazy. They are very different. Calm means you are focused, controlled, and aware. Lazy means you are distracted, unmotivated, and checked out. This is why calm must also be paired with confidence and commitment. Otherwise, you can quickly look lazy.

Confident

Confidence doesn't mean arrogance. Nobody wants to follow someone who is cocky or full of themselves. Overconfidence makes it hard to connect with your students because you're too focused on yourself. To connect, you must set aside your ego and focus on the student.

At the same time, being filled with self-doubt is just as harmful. Students don't want to follow someone who looks unsure or weak. They want to feel like you can guide them to the next level. Real confidence gives them that assurance.

Here's the key: whether it's arrogance or insecurity, it always comes down to how you make the other person *feel*. Overconfidence makes others feel small and unimportant. Insecurity makes others feel unsure. People want to be around those who inspire them and make them feel their best. That's what presence is all about.

Committed

Being committed isn't about how you look or sound. It's about what's inside you. Are you willing to follow through and help the student grow? Will you confront bad behavior right away? Will you give your whole heart to the class? If the answer is yes, your commitment will show. You can't fake it. Students see it and feel it. Before you step on the mat, make sure you are fully committed.

The takeaway is this: presence is not about performance—it's about influence. And to build that presence, the first step is simple: get over yourself.

GETTING OVER YOURSELF

Now that you know you must present yourself as calm, confident, and committed, you may still hit a barrier. The first time you lead a class, you might feel nervous, and that's normal. The goal is to overcome those nerves quickly. The best way is to show up prepared and know your material. Confidence comes from competence. Confidence is built through practice, role-playing, and repetition. The more you teach, the more naturally calm you will become.

But what if you've practiced, role-played, and memorized your material, and you still feel anxious? You're not alone. Public speaking is one of the top fears people have, often second only to death. The reasons include fear of judgment, fear of failure, and social anxiety. But all of these fears come down to one root cause: caring too much about what other people think.

Here's proof. Take someone afraid of public speaking and put them in an empty room. Ask them to give their speech out loud. Almost always, they'll do it with no problem. The only difference is the lack of people. This shows that the fear comes from worrying about what others think.

Common thoughts often sound like this:

- "What will they think if I stutter or mess up?"

- "What if I forget my speech? They'll think I'm a failure."

- "They think my voice sounds funny. They think I look funny."

- "I'm not important enough to be up here."

I know these thoughts well because I've struggled with them my whole life. Growing up, everything I did—how I dressed, what I said, how I acted—was filtered through how I thought others would view me. It was exhausting. But then I realized one powerful truth: people don't care nearly as much as you think they do.

Yes, sometimes people notice how you look or sound, but it doesn't last. They quickly move on with their own lives. Why? Because people care more about themselves than about you. That's not an insult—it's human nature. We all think about ourselves first in order to survive. Once I accepted this, I began to live more freely.

When you care too much about what others think, you hold back your true self—the unique personality God gave you. But when you shift your focus to serving others, your presence changes. That's what leadership is about.

This doesn't mean you should say or do whatever you want without considering others. Respect and service must come first. If you try to live by the Bible as I do, you already have a foundation for this. And even if you don't, you likely believe respect and serving others matter. You wouldn't be reading this book otherwise.

So, how do you stop caring so much about what strangers think? First, accept that it's actually a form of narcissism. Narcissism, in this context, is believing you're so important that everyone is paying attention to you. The truth is, they aren't. People are mostly thinking about themselves. The answer is simple: get over yourself.

That's what I had to do, and it changed everything. When you stop focusing on yourself and start focusing on serving God, serving others, and giving your best to the task at hand, you stop caring what people think. That's when life opens up.

Now, I'll be honest—it's easier said than done. We're wired to care at least a little about what others think. It's a battle we all fight daily. But here's something that has helped me, a tool I call the 'Then What Method.'

For example, if I feel anxious about speaking in front of a crowd, I go through the scenarios:

- "What if I forget half my speech?" I might turn red, stumble, and people might laugh.

- Then what? They might tell others.

- Then what? Maybe someone will post about it online.

- Then what? A few people laugh, then they move on.

Do you see how silly it becomes as you play it out? Almost always, the worst-case scenario isn't nearly as bad as your mind makes it. Even if something embarrassing happens, people move on quickly.

So let today be the day you begin living differently. Stop worrying about what others think. Focus on showing up prepared, giving your best, and serving those in front of you. That's the first step toward becoming the kind of leader people want to follow.

MASTERING YOUR PRESENCE

Let's start with your posture. Your goal is to show calmness while staying alert. Keep your head in a neutral position, with your chin not too high or too low. Tilting your chin up comes across as tense or arrogant. Tilting it down makes you look unsure or disconnected.

Your shoulders should be relaxed, not raised or stiff. Keep them slightly back but not forced, or you'll look uptight. Rounded shoulders that slump forward make you look insecure. This often comes from weak back muscles. If that's you, start strengthening your back—it will improve your posture.

Your arms should rest naturally at your sides. If you need to do something with them, place them behind your back. Avoid crossing them in front of your chest, which looks arrogant, or clasping them in front of your legs, which looks nervous. Don't fidget or cross your fingers, which communicates anxiety.

Your spine should keep a natural "S-curve." Don't over-arch, which looks tense, and don't slouch, which looks insecure and low energy. Neutral is the goal.

Eye contact also matters. Too little looks avoidant and unsure. Too much can overwhelm students and cause them to shut down. Later, we'll cover exactly how to use eye contact, but for now, remember this: it's one of the most powerful tools of your presence. Keep your eyes calm—too wide looks tense, too narrow looks tired. Don't stare at the floor while walking; it signals insecurity. Constantly darting your eyes makes you look nervous.

Your face should be relaxed, with a neutral or slight smile. If your resting face looks angry, worried, or upset, that's something to work on. People often told me I looked mad when I wasn't—I just carried a tense expression. Now, before stepping in front of others, I make a conscious effort to relax my face and smile.

The two areas that matter most are your eyebrows and mouth. Pinched eyebrows look angry or worried. Raised eyebrows look anxious or surprised, so save that for moments of praise. Keep them neutral most of the time. Pressed lips look tense or frustrated. Keep your mouth relaxed, ideally with a soft smile.

From the moment you walk into a room, onto the mats, or into the presence of your students, the show has begun. Every movement adds to the judgment your students form about you. Since your goal is to appear relaxed and confident, your movements should be smooth and deliberate. Walking too fast makes you look anxious or unprepared, which lowers student confidence. Whether you're sitting, standing, or picking something up, move with intention. Save quick movements for when you want to spark energy or give praise.

Energy is another key factor. What you feel inside will not always be what you show outside. Internally, your goal should be high energy so you can give your best effort. But externally, your presence should show neutral energy—not high, not low. Students feed off what you bring. If you bring high energy to a group of already high-energy four-year-olds, it's like throwing gasoline on a fire. It's easier to raise energy when needed than to bring it down once a class is overstimulated.

Aim for neutral energy: calm and steady. This makes you seem a little mysterious and unpredictable, which helps with discipline. Students won't know exactly how you'll respond, especially when they test boundaries. Later, we'll go deeper into the importance of being unpredictable.

CRAFTING YOUR VOICE

The foundation of the MENTOR Method is the voice. Your voice is the main tool you use to reach your students. If you were going into battle, would you want a pocketknife or a broadsword? Many smart, capable leaders fall short because their voice is still a pocketknife. They master the material but forget the most important part: the delivery.

Your voice is how you deliver knowledge. A well-crafted voice not only commands attention but is also pleasant to hear. It becomes the key that opens the door to the minds of your students. An undeveloped voice, however, gets rejected because it doesn't have that key. The goal is for your listener not just to hear your message, but to want to hear it with anticipation for more.

Volume

Volume is how loud or quiet you are. Most people don't speak loudly enough, often because they care too much about what others think. Some don't even like the sound of their own voice. But when you don't project, you sound insecure or timid. Worse, students might not hear you at all. If you're going to speak, make it count.

Speaking too loudly can also backfire. It may come across as aggressive or even painful, which causes students to retreat. In my experience, more leaders need to increase their volume than decrease it—but both matter.

True volume comes from your diaphragm, not your throat. Tightening your throat makes your voice harsh, like yelling. Instead, breathe through your nose, fill your belly with air, and push your stomach in as you speak. That pressure gives you volume without strain. Good posture also helps your lungs reach their full potential.

Leadership isn't about always being loud. The skill is knowing when to raise and when to lower your volume. Use more volume for group instructions. Lower it when you want students to lean in and listen closely. That unpredictability keeps attention.

Tone

Tone is the color of your voice—the emotion behind the sound. It's the main "how" in the phrase: It's not what you say, it's how you say it.

Tone comes from a mix of air and vocal cords. Too much air makes it weak. Too much throat makes it harsh. Both have a place. For comfort or compassion, use a softer, airy tone. For authority, lean more toward the edge.

On a scale from 1 (all air) to 10 (all edge), aim for 7. That balance commands respect without yelling, sounds trustworthy, and reaches students clearly.

Try this: Say "AH" for a few seconds, shifting from airy to edgy. Find the sweet spot at 7. Then say, "I'm happy to be here" in that tone—strong but relaxed, friendly but confident. This is the tone you'll use most often.

Pitch

Pitch is the note of your voice—high, low, or in between. High pitch shows excitement, playfulness, or curiosity. Low pitch shows authority and seriousness.

Too many high-pitched sounds are overwhelming. Too much low pitch feels dull. The goal is contrast.

Save high pitch for moments of praise or excitement, so your words feel powerful. Most of the time, use a lower pitch—around 4 out of 10—to establish authority. Test your range by seeing how high and low you can go without cracking. The more range, the more tools you have.

Pace

Pace is the speed of your words. Some people speak too fast, others too slow. Great speakers use both—on purpose.

Fast pace shows energy and helps move through boring material. Slow pace emphasizes big ideas. The key is variety. Too fast all the time, feels anxious. Too slow all the time feels dull. Match your pace to your students.

One of the most powerful tools is the purposeful pause. Silence, when used well, makes students lean in. At first, silence will feel uncomfortable, but learn to embrace it. Pauses work best after faster speech, like a steep drop after a climb.

Use pauses to:

- Address unwanted behavior
- Emphasize a key point
- Add dramatic effect

Clarity

Above all, your voice must deliver your message. This means speaking with clarity—pronouncing each word so students understand.

Clarity comes from enunciation, which means sounding out every syllable and consonant. Slow down and open your mouth more. Practice making consonants crisp—like sharp "T's" and "S's" that cut through the air.

Tongue twisters help:

- Please pack the purple pens properly.
- Tom took ten tiny turtles to town.
- Peter picked a peck of pickled peppers.
- Silly students stay sharp by stepping strong and standing still.

Also, cut out filler words such as "um", "uh", "like", and "you know". They weaken your presence. People use them because they fear silence, but silence can be powerful.

Melody

Melody is what happens when you combine all the building blocks. It's the rhythm, flow, and music of your voice.

Think of your favorite song. Why do you like it? Because it has variety: different notes, tempos, and surprises. If it stayed the same, it would get boring. Your voice works the same way.

The melody should shift depending on your audience. For young kids, be more dramatic. For teens, tone it down, or you'll sound fake. For adults, focus on clarity and confidence.

Think of each sentence as a canvas. Use volume, tone, pitch, and pace to paint it. Then pause before the next one.

Protecting Your Voice

Your voice is a muscle, and like any muscle, it can get tired. Speaking too long or too loudly makes one hoarse. That's your body warning you.

Protect your voice by breathing through your nose, which moistens the air before it reaches your vocal cords. Stay hydrated. Avoid yelling or straining for long periods. Use your diaphragm, pace yourself, and rest when needed.

The stronger and healthier your voice, the more effective you'll be as a leader.

PART 3

THE FOUR C'S OF EARNING RESPECT

Before you can earn trust, you must first earn respect. As we've established, the MENTOR Method prioritizes respect over being liked. Now let's look at how respect is earned through four key actions, each starting with the letter C.

Positional authority matters because it gives you a platform to set and enforce expectations. A common misunderstanding is that positional authority is gained through force or intimidation. While this can be true, it is not the right path. Leading through fear is not only in bad taste, but it is ineffective because it relies on extrinsic motivation. The better way is to earn your students' respect so that they want to follow you. Let's look at the four C's of earning respect.

Confrontation

Positional authority from your presence and uniform won't last long by itself. The next step is to set expectations and confront students who do not meet them. Confrontation is the fastest way to earn deeper respect. Presence and attire might give students an idea of who you are, but confrontation shows them exactly who you are inside.

When you directly address a student who is not meeting expectations, the thought that they might get away with poor behavior quickly disappears. Even if you only confront one student, everyone watching will understand that you will hold them accountable, too. Not being afraid to confront is one of the most powerful skills a leader can have. Many people struggle with it because it feels personal or awkward. But the quicker you get past that hesitation, the quicker you will grow as a teacher and leader.

Always confront with respect and professionalism. Not only is this the right thing to do, but it also models the behavior you want to see in your students. More importantly, it shows that you can handle leading the group. The moment you display negative emotion, you communicate that leading them is more than you can manage. Always strive to maintain a positive attitude, no matter the student's behavior.

Consistency

After showing that you will confront unmet expectations, you must also prove that you will do it consistently. Nothing destroys respect faster than inconsistency. If you say you will follow through with a consequence but then fail to do it, students will lose respect. Once they believe they can get away with breaking the rules, your authority fades.

Consistency builds trust because students know what to expect and feel secure in the learning environment. It reduces confusion by creating a clear path to success. It models discipline, which everyone respects. It also eliminates favoritism, since consistent enforcement shows fairness. Finally, consistent routines and repeated practice make it easier for students to learn and retain skills.

Competence

Confronting unmet expectations earns respect. Being consistent keeps it. But showing competence earns the deepest level of respect. Students respect instructors who know what they are teaching. If you want to become a world-class chef, you want to learn from a world-class chef.

This does not mean you must physically perform every skill you teach. Many elite coaches cannot perform the skills they teach at a high level. What matters most is your knowledge and your ability to guide the student toward their goals. Most students care less about whether you can perform the skill and more about how you can help them improve.

You demonstrate competence by speaking with confidence and clarity. If you stumble or hesitate, students start to question whether you know the material. Conflicting or contradicting statements can also cause them to lose faith. This is why preparation matters. Know your material forward and backward. Glancing at bullet points is fine, but if you rely heavily on notes or a device, you are not ready. The goal is to reach a flow state when teaching, where you and your students are fully engaged. Don't take shortcuts—earn their respect through mastery.

Character

Respect from position and competence is important, but the deepest level of respect comes from your character. This is the kind of respect that can last a lifetime. The teachers I remember most were not just skilled—they had solid character. They carried themselves with honor and humility. They treated people with fairness and kindness. And what I saw in public matched how they lived in private.

Nothing destroys respect faster than discovering someone you admired was living a double life. This is why your role as a leader, teacher, or mentor must be taken seriously. Your students may look up to you and want to be like you. You don't need to be perfect—none of us are—but you should strive for excellence in character.

When you make a mistake, admit it quickly. Apologize with humility. Many believe apologizing shows weakness, but the truth is, it builds respect. Students forgive quickly when they see genuine humility. What destroys respect is making excuses or blaming others. Even small errors, like using the wrong term, are opportunities to model humility. Just say, "I apologize, that's not what I meant," and move on.

PART 3: THE FOUR C'S OF EARNING RESPECT

Your students are always watching, both inside and outside the classroom. The respect that comes from strong character is not easy to earn, but it is worth the effort. When your students respect your character, the impact you leave on their lives will last long after the lessons are over.

PART 4

THE INSTRUCTOR TRIANGLE

Imagine a three-legged stool. If one leg is missing or weak, the stool will tip over. Teaching works the same way. The three legs of your stool are Connect, Catch, and Coach. Without all three, your teaching will wobble.

Many instructors lean too heavily on one leg. Some only try to connect by being friendly. Others only try to catch mistakes without building relationships. Some focus only on coaching by giving corrections and drills. The problem is that each leg on its own is incomplete. For your teaching to stand strong, you must balance all three.

Connect

The first leg is Connect. Connection is what allows you to reach the student in the first place. If they don't feel seen, they won't listen. Connection can be as simple as making eye contact, asking about their day, or showing interest in their life. For younger children, this might mean asking about their favorite game or what they had for lunch. For teens, it could mean asking about a sport, class, or interest. For adults, it might be asking about work or family.

Connection builds trust. When students feel that you care about them as people, not just performers, they are more open to your instruction. But connection alone is not enough. If you only connect, you risk becoming more of a friend than a leader. That's why you also need to catch.

Catch

The second leg is Catch. This is your ability to notice correct and incorrect behavior and call it out in the moment. Timing is everything here. The faster you catch it, the more powerful the impact.

Catching the correct behavior gives the student confidence and reinforces progress. "Great job snapping that kick right when I said 'go.'" Catching the incorrect behavior shows the student you are paying attention and will hold them accountable. "That was too slow. Let's reset and try again."

The key is balance. If you only catch mistakes, you create frustration. If you only catch the good, you allow bad habits to grow. The most effective instructors catch both quickly, clearly, and consistently.

Coach

The third leg is Coach. This is where you guide the student to the next level. Coaching goes beyond catching. When you coach, you show the "how." You explain, demonstrate, and give feedback that helps them improve.

Coaching means breaking things down into steps, giving adjustments, and pushing students toward their potential. This is where your competence shows. If you don't know the material or can't explain it clearly, coaching falls apart.

The danger here is that some instructors only coach: talking endlessly, giving long lectures, and over-explaining. This loses the student's attention. That's why it must stay balanced with connect and catch.

Balance in Action

Let's look at what this balance looks like in practice.

- Martial arts class: You connect by greeting each student by name. You catch by praising the ones who lined up fast and confronting the ones who were slow. You coach by adjusting their stance or kick to make it sharper.

- Classroom: You connect by asking about a student's weekend. You catch by pointing out who responded quickly when your hand went up and who did not. You coach by clearly explaining the steps of a math problem.

- Parenting at home: You connect by sharing a laugh with your child before school. You catch them by noticing they forgot to put their dish away, and you remind them right away. You coach by showing them how to fold their laundry correctly.

Each of these examples shows all three legs working together. Without connection, the student might ignore you. Without catching, they won't take you seriously. Without coaching, they won't know how to improve.

The Power of Catching in the Moment

Of the three legs, catching is often the one that separates average instructors from great ones. Average instructors notice but wait too long to respond. Great instructors act quickly. They catch the moment while it's still fresh, before the lesson is lost.

If a child responds slowly to your command, address it right then. If a youth gives half effort, call it out in the moment. If an adult misunderstands the instruction, clarify immediately. The quicker you catch it, the more likely it will change.

The Complete Stool

When all three legs—Connect, Catch, and Coach—are strong, your teaching is steady. You build trust, you hold standards, and you guide growth. If one leg is missing, your influence wobbles. The stool tips.

The Instructor Triangle is the foundation. The MENTOR Method gives you the step-by-step process. Together, they make you both balanced and effective.

Takeaways

- Connect builds trust.

- Catch holds students accountable.

- Coach guides them to the next level.

- Catching in the moment is what separates average from great instructors.

- When all three are balanced, your teaching stands strong like a sturdy stool.

PART 5

ENGAGEMENT IS EVERYTHING

Now that we know the importance of setting the objective first, the next step is to transfer the information to the student. Sounds easy, right? Wrong. If you have ever taught anyone, especially children, you know it is not as simple as it sounds. This is especially true when the student does not naturally have an interest in what you are teaching.

The hardest truth for many teachers to accept is this: the student is the only one who holds the key to the door of their mind. No matter how hard the teacher knocks or tries to push the door open, only the student can unlock it. The student must first choose to receive the information the teacher is sending. What causes the student to open that door? Engagement.

Engagement is the key that unlocks the mind of the student. No engagement, no access to the mind. And without access to the mind, no skill or knowledge can be transferred. This is why engagement must always stay front and center in the mind of the teacher. You can have the best intentions and care deeply about the subject, but if the student is not engaged, all your time and energy will be wasted.

What Sparks Engagement?

Engagement begins the moment the student feels a personal connection to what is being taught. That connection can come from curiosity or the excitement of taking on a challenge. It might be as simple as wanting to have fun, or it could be more serious, like wanting to improve their side kick to win first place in a tournament. Either way, the connection always comes down to how it benefits the student.

Once you know the student's end goal, you can work backward to spark their engagement. This is why it is so important to get to know the student as quickly as possible. Not only to uncover their goal but also to build trust. Without trust, it is very hard to spark engagement.

Think of a clown at a birthday party. The kids may be engaged and laughing from the show, but could the clown suddenly start teaching them a skill? Probably not. Most of the kids would be unsure or even scared if the clown came close. Why? Because no trust was built first. The type of engagement you want is deeper: based on curiosity, connection, and a drive to reach their personal goal.

Here's the key point: the engagement you want from your student is not the same as the engagement of a child watching a clown. That's only entertainment. While you may grab attention by being fun and exciting, it should not stop there.

The Danger of Entertainment-Only Teaching

A common mistake adults make when teaching kids is thinking they must entertain the entire time. The problem is that the child's motivation then relies entirely on the teacher's performance. Once the entertainment stops, the motivation fades.

This is called extrinsic motivation, which is motivation based on outside factors.

The problem with relying on extrinsic motivation is that the student does not truly care about the skill or knowledge being taught. They just go through the motions, and the lesson does not stick. Another problem is that being the "entertainment" all the time will quickly burn you out. You only have so much energy, and if you teach multiple classes in a day, you will wear down fast.

The better kind of engagement is intrinsic motivation—motivation that comes from within. The student is curious and wants to learn more. They are not motivated to be entertained but to reach a personal goal or desire.

Intrinsic Motivation Based on Age

This inner drive changes as children grow:

- Six and younger: Their motivation comes mainly from receiving praise from a trusted adult, such as a parent or teacher. Trust and security are critical at this age.

- Ages 7–12: Their motivation comes from a mix of wanting praise and wanting to reach personal goals. They begin to see the teacher as a guide who can help them get where they want to go.

- Age 13 and older: Their motivation shifts more toward self-evaluation and personal goals. They see praise as feedback on what they're doing right or wrong, not just something that makes them feel good.

While trust is always important, how you build it changes by age. For the very young, trust gives them a sense of safety. For older kids, trust is about proving you can actually guide them to where they want to go.

As they become preteens and teens, trust tips even more toward believing you have the knowledge to help them reach their goals. At this age, they may not need as much emotional security from you, but they must believe in your skill and ability to guide them.

Motivation Based on Social Acceptance

Why do students want to reach their personal goals? Often, it is because they want the approval of their peers.

At around age six, children start to care what their peers think. As they grow into their teen years, peer approval can become one of their strongest motivators. This is important to understand because it helps you keep engagement high.

For example, you can have teenage students work in pairs. They will often give more effort because they don't want to look bad in front of their peers. At this stage, social acceptance may matter more than gaining praise from the teacher.

It can be tough to accept, but don't take it personally. Keep the bigger goal in mind. As they grow into young adults, they will start to care less about peer approval and more about their own standards. If you have earned their trust and respect, they will accept your instruction and feedback openly.

Speaking of respect, let's now look at where that fits into the equation.

PART 6

NEVER FORGET THE OBJECTIVE

Before you start teaching a lesson, class, or session, you must establish a clear objective in your mind. What are you trying to accomplish today? What needs to happen for you to feel like you made real progress with your student or students?

The objective should always be clear and measurable. Without it, you risk falling into the trap of just doing things to fill time. This often leads to burnout, because without a strong reason for what you're doing, the hard days will make you want to quit.

It's also important for the student to know the objective and how it affects them. A student is far more motivated when they understand, for example, that the only way they'll earn their next stripe or belt is by being able to perform a technique properly.

Short-Term Goals Tied to Long-Term Goals

The goal you set today should always connect to a bigger goal in the future. The farther ahead you aim, the more powerful today's objective becomes.

At Ko Martial Arts, our bigger goal is to help students become leaders of themselves and then of others. To make that happen, we aim to keep students enrolled with us through high school graduation. If a child starts with us at age three, that objective won't be accomplished for at least 15 years.

From this, we can identify three key objectives:

1. Keep students enrolled through high school graduation.

2. Help students become leaders of themselves.

3. Help students become leaders of others.

Out of these three, which is the most important? Staying enrolled. Why? Because if a student quits early, we lose the chance to accomplish the last two. Only in the later years of high school can we truly shape students into leaders of themselves and others.

So, what does that mean for today's objective? It's simple: don't let the student quit.

Keeping the Bigger Picture in Mind

It's important not to misunderstand this. I'm not saying you should let students do whatever they want just to keep them around. Students come with the intention of gaining knowledge, not just passing the time.

Your job is to set an objective for the day and work to accomplish it. One goal we should always have is that progress has been made. Even if the progress is little, forward motion is what matters.

For example, if today's objective was for the student to perform a sequence of three techniques, but they came in tired or in a bad mood, you may not hit all three. But if the student started knowing none of the techniques and left being able to do two, that's still a win. Progress was made.

Without setting your objective ahead of time, you have nothing to measure progress against. You won't know if you succeeded or not.

Goals Within Goals

Daily objectives should connect upward:

- Today's goal supports this week's goal.

- This week supports this quarter.

- This quarter supports this year.

- This year supports the bigger goals, like earning a black belt.

At Ko Martial Arts, earning a black belt takes about three years. That goal is broken down into quarterly, weekly, and daily objectives. Every class should focus on something that moves the student closer to a black belt while also tying back to the overarching goal of staying enrolled through high school graduation.

The True Objective of Teaching

No matter your field, as a coach, teacher, instructor, or professor, the true objective is to transfer a skill, knowledge, concept, or ability to the student. You know you've succeeded when the student can recite, understand, teach, or perform what was taught on their own, without your help.

It doesn't count if you still have to assist them. Independence is the measure of success.

At Ko Martial Arts, while our overarching goal is to keep students with us through high school, our daily responsibility is to transfer skills, knowledge, and character to them as effectively as possible.

SYSTEMS OF PROGRESS

A great method without a system will eventually collapse. The MENTOR Method gives you the framework for how to teach, but systems are what keep it consistent across days, weeks, and even years. Without systems, you're left relying on memory, mood, or chance—and students can feel the difference.

Progress must be visible, not just felt. When students and parents can see the steps forward, motivation stays high. When instructors can track those same steps, accountability stays strong. Systems make both possible.

A system of progress doesn't have to be complicated. At its core, it answers three questions:

1. What is the expectation?

2. How is it measured?

3. How is it communicated?

When those answers are clear, students know what to aim for, instructors know how to guide them, and parents know how to support them.

Some systems track skills through stripes, belts, or levels. Others track behavior, attendance, or leadership growth. The exact system you use matters less than this: it must be consistent, transparent, and easy to follow.

The MENTOR Method works best when it is tied to a visible system of progress. It turns abstract concepts into something concrete. It gives students a sense of achievement, instructors a roadmap for what to teach next, and parents confidence that real growth is happening.

Think of systems as the scaffolding that supports the house you're building with the MENTOR Method. Without them, the structure weakens. With them, the house stands tall for years.

Now, before we talk about how the MENTOR Method framework works in the next section, you need to master the fundamental tools that make any teaching method work: communication, praise, and drill design. Your voice is the most powerful tool you have.

PART 7

THE MENTOR METHOD FRAMEWORK

Before we dive into the MENTOR Method step by step, it's important to understand what it is—and what it is not.

The MENTOR Method is not a set of tricks. It is not a quick fix for keeping kids under control. It is a framework that helps you guide students from where they are to where they need to be.

Every letter in the word MENTOR represents a stage in this process. Each stage builds on the one before it, like bricks in a wall. If you skip one, the wall weakens. But when you follow the sequence, you create structure, consistency, and momentum that your students can feel.

Think of it like climbing a ladder. Each rung gets you higher, but only if you step on the rung below it first. If you try to skip too many, you risk falling. The MENTOR Method makes sure you and your students always have a firm step beneath you.

This framework works because it creates order without crushing creativity. It keeps expectations clear without becoming rigid. It builds trust and discipline while leaving room for growth. In short, it gives you a map.

Without a map, teaching feels scattered and random. You may know where you want your students to end up, but without clear steps, they often get lost along the way. The MENTOR Method removes that guesswork. It gives you a tested path to follow.

In the chapters ahead, we'll break down each stage of the framework, starting with Measure. You'll see how each stage connects to the next, and how the entire sequence creates a system that works in any classroom, on any field, or in any training hall.

But before you move forward, remember this: the framework is only as strong as the person using it. If you skip steps, rush the process, or apply it without consistency, it will not work. But if you commit to it fully, you will see your students transform—one step, one stage, one brick at a time.

MEASURE

M stands for **Measure**, the first step of the MENTOR Method. Before you can start teaching, you must know where the student is. You have to meet them at their level.

Too often, instructors start at the wrong point. They choose a place based on their own plan instead of the student's ability. The problem is that the student has to skip steps to keep up. When this happens, they don't fully learn the skill. They get frustrated, and their motivation drops. I call this gap the **tension gap**.

The tension gap creates friction. The instructor feels disappointed because the student isn't performing as expected. That frustration often shows through body language or tone. The student, already nervous because the skill feels too hard, now feels even more pressure. Both spiral into frustration.

This can be avoided by measuring correctly and setting the right expectation for the student's starting point. Frustration happens when expectations don't match reality. Instead of holding onto the wrong expectation, adjust it. Modify the expectation and don't get frustrated.

You might think lowering expectations is letting the student off easy. It's not. Starting too high discourages students and often makes them want to quit. And if they quit, no progress is made.

But when you measure correctly, success becomes possible. Imagine a student must learn steps A, B, C, and D, each harder than the last. If they already know A, start with B. Because B is only a little harder, the student is more likely to succeed. That success builds confidence and motivation. It also gives you a chance to praise them, which fuels momentum.

Why is Measure so important? Because students can only commit to their best efforts if they think they can achieve success. When the starting point is too far ahead, students lose focus because the challenge feels huge. From 'I'd like to improve' to 'Just let me finish this.' Getting it right keeps the door to intrinsic motivation open. As soon as they think they can succeed at the task, they lean in. As soon as they think they can't, they check out.

The end goal is always progress. Even the smallest step forward matters. What you never want is no progress—or worse, moving backward. Your role is to create opportunities for forward movement. Some days the steps will be big. Other days they will be small. Either way, progress must continue.

That's why Measure comes first. Once you know the true starting point, the next step is to **Establish the expectation**.

Here's what measuring looks like in real time. I'm teaching a new student, Fred, his first front kick. The measurement happens immediately: he's brand new and knows nothing about how to do a front kick. That tells me exactly where to start. Instead of asking him to attempt a full kick, I begin with one simple request: "Pull your knee up high." He tries, and I immediately praise him: "Yes! That's exactly what I wanted to see."

If I had started by saying, "Chamber your knee at 90 degrees, keep your base foot planted, extend through the ball of your foot, and re-chamber before setting down," I would have overwhelmed him. He's not ready for that level of detail.

Instead, I measure what he just showed me and start with one adjustment: "Great try. This time, pull your knee up higher before you kick.' That's all. One change. He tries again—this time his knee comes up better, but his supporting foot turns out. I notice, but I don't correct it yet. Why? Because he's still working on the first piece.

After three or four kicks with a higher chamber, I add the next layer: "Now keep that same high knee, and point your toes forward on the foot that's on the ground." He adjusts. Now he's building.

This is measuring in action. I met Fred where he was, not where I wanted him to be. Each step was achievable. Each success built momentum. By the end of five minutes, his kick looked sharper than when we started... not perfect, but better. And more importantly, he felt capable.

Takeaways

- Always start by finding the student's true level.

- Avoid creating a tension gap—set expectations that match reality.

- Lowering expectations is not a weakness—it is the best way to create confidence and progress.

- Small steps forward build momentum; skipped steps create frustration.

- Progress, not perfection, is the goal of Measure.

ESTABLISH

The next step in the MENTOR Method is to **Establish** the expectation. But before you set it, you must first make a connection with the student. This happens through your presence and by building rapport.

Make eye contact. Ask questions. If you know them well, ask about their life: "How was your birthday party last week?" If you don't know them as well, ask something lighter: "What's your favorite dessert?" Either way, show real interest. Don't glance away while they talk, or they'll feel you don't care.

This connection helps the student feel seen. But it's only the first step. If you stop here, the student may see you as a friend. You are not their friend—

you are their leader, coach, or guide. You prove this through your presence and later by holding them accountable when expectations are missed.

Once the connection is made, you decide what the expectation will be. Time and group size matter. A one-on-one session allows more focus than a large class. Always think about these factors before setting the expectation.

The expectation must be realistic. Sometimes you'll set it too high. That's okay—you can quickly adjust it down. It's better to start lower and raise it later than start too high and have to lower it after failure. Starting low builds momentum. Success at the first step gives the student confidence to move to the next. Starting too high creates defeat and discouragement.

Every expectation has two parts: a **prompt** and a **response**. The prompt is your request. The response is the student's action. For example: "When I say sit, you will sit quickly." That's clear and simple. Don't make it complex with too many prompts at once. That only sets the student up to fail.

If your long-term goal is for students to move quickly to any command, don't start with them all. Begin with one: maybe standing up quickly. Once that's solid, add sitting down. Then add lining up. One step at a time is far more effective than asking for everything at once.

Over time, if you keep setting the same expectations, students should come back already meeting them. You say "sit," and they do it quickly because they've practiced it enough. Of course, some will still need reminders, which we'll cover in the last step of the method.

When you set the expectation, communicate it clearly. Speak slowly, clearly, and loud enough to be heard. Be detailed enough to explain the important parts, but not so detailed that it becomes confusing. Keep eye contact. If it's a group, scan the room so every student feels included. If someone isn't paying attention, correct it right away, then continue. You only have a short window before attention slips.

Don't just state the expectation, confirm they heard it. Have them repeat it back. This makes it stick in their mind and avoids tension later.

One additional crucial aspect: clarity creates choice. When there is no clarity in the expectation, they can't even think of excellence because they can't see it. But if there is clarity in their expectation, they have the choice to say, "Do I want to live up to the expectation or not?" This is where intrinsic motivation is. You're not compelling them to meet the expectation; you're pointing out to them the target to hit.

Once the student has repeated the expectation, the next step is to **Notice** progress.

Takeaways

- Connect before you correct—rapport builds trust for expectations to stick.

- Every expectation must be realistic—start small, then raise the bar.

- Clear communication requires simplicity: one prompt, one response.

- Confirm they understand by having them repeat it back.

- Small wins build momentum; overwhelming students breaks it.

NOTICE

The next step in the MENTOR Method is to **notice** when progress has been made. This step fuels the student's motivation to keep going. The progress does not have to be big—it can be very small. What matters is that it is noticed and acknowledged.

Don't just notice silently. Call it out in a positive way. This praise reinforces the behavior you want. In a group, it also encourages others to copy that behavior.

Students know when your excitement is real. Show it with your face, your body, and your voice. Smile, make eye contact, and raise the pitch of your voice slightly. Let your body naturally show energy. Remember—it's not just what you say, but how you say it.

Speed matters. The sooner you praise, the stronger the connection between the action and the reward. If you wait too long, the student forgets what they just did. To catch it quickly, you must pay attention at all times. When you get distracted, you miss chances to reinforce the right behavior.

The Eagle Eye

To notice effectively, you must develop what I call the "Eagle Eye." An eagle can scan wide across the horizon and, at the same time, notice the smallest movement. As an instructor, you must do the same. See the whole group while also picking up on individual details.

Position yourself where you can see everyone. Don't lock in on one student for too long. Scan often. Use your peripheral vision. Rotate your focus so every student feels your attention. When possible, make eye contact with each student. This sharpens engagement and helps you catch both good and bad behavior the moment it happens.

Be Specific

When you give praise, be specific. Don't just say, "Good job!" Connect the praise to the expectation. For example, if the expectation is to kick as soon as you say "kick," your praise should be, "Good job kicking the target right when I said kick!" That links the praise directly to the behavior you want.

There will be times when no progress is made. Notice that too. But unlike praise, don't respond right away. Sometimes silence itself motivates the student. If they hear no praise, they may try harder. But don't wait too long, or engagement will drop. If progress still isn't made, reestablish the expectation. Sometimes you must simplify it so the student can succeed. That's not failure—it's part of the process.

Another reason progress may stall is a lack of connection. If the student doesn't feel seen or doesn't see you as the leader, you must go back to establish and rebuild.

Once progress is happening, the next step is to test if it continues.

Takeaways

- Noticing progress fuels motivation, even if the progress is little.

- Praise must be specific and connected directly to the expectation.

- Speed matters—catch progress immediately, or the moment is lost.

- Develop an Eagle Eye: scan the whole group while catching individual details.

- If progress stalls, use silence, reset the expectation, or rebuild the connection.

TEST

The next step in the MENTOR Method is to **Test**. Testing is when you step back to see if the student can meet the expectation with less help. Praise for little progress is no longer enough. The goal now is for the student to meet the expectation on their own.

Notice was about praising every small step. Test is about saving your praise for bigger steps. Notice was hands-on. Test is stepping back. Your prompts should become less frequent, and your speaking should return to a normal pace.

A good time to start testing is when the student can meet the expectation several times in a row with ease. If they struggle too much, go back to Notice and try again later.

Two key parts of mastery are forgetting and recall. Forgetting clears space in the brain. Recall strengthens connections and turns short-term learning into a long-term skill.

You create forgetting and recall by adding new expectations. The brain can only focus on one thing at a time, so the new expectation pushes the old one aside. Then, without warning, ask for the earlier expectation. This forces the student to recall, which deepens mastery.

Don't jump in with the answer if they struggle. Struggling is the work that makes the learning stick. Find the balance between not waiting long enough and waiting too long. The goal is for the student to strain just enough without giving up.

The less feedback you give, the better. Silence is powerful. Saying nothing while the student works gives them the space to figure it out.

Think of a baby learning to walk. At first, you hold both hands. Then you hold one. Finally, you let go but stay close. If you never let go, the baby never learns to walk. Parents often want to stop their baby from falling, but without falling, the baby never learns balance. Instructors do the same when they give the answer too quickly. It feels helpful, but it stops mastery.

A common mistake is testing too early or raising the bar too fast. This overwhelms the student. Patience is the key.

You can also test by changing the context. For example, if the expectation is to line up quickly, you may first have them line up side by side. Later, ask them to line up in multiple rows. The format changed, but the expectation— move quickly—stays the same. This shows the student that the expectation is not tied to one routine, but is a habit that applies anywhere.

This is where the shift from extrinsic to intrinsic motivation actually happens, and it's easy to miss if you're not paying attention.

In the Authoritative Method, the instructor never steps back. Students remain dependent on commands and consequences. They follow orders like "Do ten pushups. Now run a lap. Now line up." The student obeys, but only because the instructor is always there. Take the authority figure away, and the effort disappears.

In the Tippy Toe Method, the instructor steps back, but only because they have exhausted their energy tricks. When they announce, "Okay, everyone, free time!" the students scatter. They never really learned discipline; they were just responding to constant stimulation. Once that stimulation ends, so does any structure.

The MENTOR Method treats stepping back differently. It's intentional, not a result of exhaustion. The expectation has been built, the student has practiced under guidance, and now the instructor tests whether the student has internalized it. The key question is whether they will act without being prompted.

For example, I work with a group of eight-year-olds on their kicking combination. For ten minutes, I count every kick aloud: "Front kick! Side kick! Roundhouse!" They follow perfectly, but they are following me rather than owning the combination.

Then I step back a few feet, take a knee and lean in, and say, "This time, no counting. You know the combination. Show me you can do it on your own." I remain silent.

Three students completed it successfully. Two hesitate halfway. One stops completely and looks for help. Now I know exactly where each student stands. The three who succeeded are ready to observe. The two who hesitated need more time in practice. The one who froze isn't ready yet and needs more guidance.

The test isn't whether they can do it with you. It's whether they will do it without you. That is the difference between dependence and ownership.

Takeaways

- Testing shifts from constant praise to saving praise for bigger steps.

- Step back—give fewer prompts and less feedback.

- Struggle is necessary—don't give the answer too quickly.

- Forgetting and recall strengthen mastery.

- Use silence to let the student figure it out.

- Don't test too early or raise the bar too fast.

- Vary the context to show expectations apply everywhere.

- Testing prepares the student for the next step: Observe.

OBSERVE

The next step in the MENTOR Method is to **Observe**. This is where you confirm if the student has truly mastered the expectation. At this stage, they must be able to perform it on their own without any help.

During Observe, you remove all feedback and silently monitor their response. No nods, no gestures, no facial cues. Even the smallest signal can give the student false confidence. If you help even a little, the test is no longer valid.

Students often look at your face for approval. This is natural. To avoid giving away signals, you may need to look slightly away while keeping them in your peripheral vision.

In the Test phase, you held back from giving the answer too early. In Observe, you must hold back even more. You must allow the student to fail if that's the outcome. Failure is how you know whether they truly own the skill. The only time to step in is for safety. All feedback must wait until the attempt is complete.

As you observe, keep a mental list of what needs improvement. For example, if the expectation is to line up quickly, pay attention: Did they move right away, or hesitate? Did they form the line quickly, or did it take too long? Was the problem that they didn't know where to go, or that they didn't know how to space themselves? Every detail matters. These notes become the guide for what comes next.

Observe also builds confidence. Real confidence comes when students succeed fully on their own. That kind of confidence can't be handed to them. It only comes when they own the result, with both the success and the risk of failure.

Sometimes you'll see the student isn't ready. That's not failure—it's just a sign to return to Test for more practice before observing again. Students often move up and down the ladder before mastery sticks. Your role is to give the right support at the right time.

The next step, **Remind**, is where you provide small nudges to keep students on track long-term.

Takeaways

- Observe confirms true mastery without any help.

- Remove all feedback—no nods, gestures, or facial cues.

- Let failure happen—it proves ownership of the skill.

- Keep mental notes of details that need improvement.

- Real confidence comes from succeeding alone.

- If they aren't ready, return to Test and try again later.

- Mastery isn't permanent—Observe must be revisited over time.

REMIND

The final step of the MENTOR Method is **Remind**. At this stage, the student should not need any help. They should be meeting the expectation on their own, almost automatically. But the student will never fully leave this stage. Skills always fade over time, and everyone needs reminders to stay sharp. Forgetting and recalling again is part of how mastery deepens.

In Observe, you were still watching closely to confirm the expectation. In Remind, your effort is lighter because your focus is on new expectations. But you still notice when the student slips. If they miss once, you often let it go—mistakes happen. But if the mistake repeats or becomes a pattern, that's when you remind them.

Reminders should be quick and light. Don't make a big deal about them. A simple facial expression, like a raised eyebrow, can be enough. The student knows the mistake, and they know you saw it. That awareness alone often corrects the behavior. Sometimes a short question works: "I thought you knew how to perform that correctly?" or, "Do you know how to perform that correctly?" Even though you know the answer, the question nudges them to self-correct.

Think of Remind as a gentle nudge back onto the path. In Test, you were walking right beside them. In Notice, you were close but gave them a little more space. In Observe, you stepped even farther back. In Remind, you're not following closely at all—you're watching from a distance and stepping in only when needed. And because no one stays perfect forever, this stage never ends.

Sometimes, if a student keeps slipping, you may need to return to earlier steps. If they miss often, go back to Establish and make sure the expectation is clear. This moment belongs in the process and helps move things forward.. Some students need to revisit steps many times. Patience is required. If you let frustration show, progress slows.

Think of yourself as the CRO—the Chief Reminding Officer. How many times should you remind? As many as it takes. There is no set limit. Too many instructors stop reminding because they feel they've done it enough. That mindset doesn't work. Real growth often takes dozens or even hundreds of reminders before mastery becomes natural.

The key is to remind in a way that is respectful, positive, and steady. Reminders are not about showing frustration. They are about keeping students on track so they keep growing.

Now that we've covered all the phases of the MENTOR Method, let's look at how they connect through the picture of building a brick house.

Takeaways

- Remind keeps students sharp—skills always fade without it.

- Quick, light reminders work best—facial expressions or short questions.

- One mistake can slide, but repeated mistakes must be addressed.

- Think of it as a gentle nudge, not a lecture.

- Some students may need to revisit earlier steps—this is normal, not failure.

- Be the Chief Reminding Officer—remind as many times as needed.

- Always give reminders with respect, patience, and positivity.

BUILDING YOUR HOUSE OF EXPECTATIONS

Now that you understand each phase of the MENTOR Method, let's look at how these phases work together in real time. Think of each expectation you set as a brick in a house. Measure tells you where to place the first brick. Establish shows you how to lay it properly. Notice confirms it's secure. Test checks if it can bear weight. Observe ensures it stays in place without your hand on it. And Remind keeps you checking back as you build higher. The MENTOR Method isn't just six separate steps—it's a complete construction process.

This is how you guide your students toward the end goal—one expectation at a time. Each one is placed with precision. You don't forget about the earlier ones. You revisit them when needed. A house can be built with broken bricks, but that is not the kind of house you want to build. You want to build a house that can withstand pressure and also one that you are proud of. The kind of house that others notice right away, even if they don't understand architecture. To do this, you must become a world-class architect of expectations.

Let me walk you through how this house actually gets built, brick by brick.

It's the first class of the day. Fifteen students, ages 6 to 10, come in. I start observing immediately. Who is bouncing off the walls? Who stands quietly? Who is watching to see what comes next?

Brick one: I raise my hand. Some students stop talking right away, but others keep chattering. I wait. Five seconds. Ten seconds. Eventually, the room goes quiet. I lower my hand and say calmly, "When my hand goes up, you have three seconds to be silent. Let's try again." I raise my hand. This time it takes seven seconds. Improvement, but not enough. Third attempt—four seconds. I stop to praise the first responders. "Mia and James, excellent— you were ready in two seconds." The others want that recognition. Fourth attempt—two seconds for the whole class. That first brick is set.

Brick two: "Line up on the red tape, one arm's length apart, standing tall." They move into position, but it's sloppy. Some students touch each other. Two face the wrong way. I stop them and demonstrate proper posture—shoulders back, eyes forward, arms at sides. "Try again." This time, it's better. I walk the line, adjusting posture with quick, calm corrections. "Shoulders back. Chin level. Perfect." Brick two is in place.

Brick three: "When I say bow, bend forward with your hands at your sides and hold for two seconds. Ready? Bow." Half the class follows correctly. The rest rush through. I reset them. "Too fast. A respectful bow takes two full seconds. Let's count it together. Bow—one, two—up." Everyone holds it this time. I praise the group: "Much better. That's the standard."

Only eight minutes into class, and three expectations are already set. My house is taking shape. But I don't move to brick four until the first three are solid. If someone's hand-raise response falters while practicing bows, I stop and reset. "Wait—I didn't see three-second focus when my hand went up. Let's make sure that the brick is solid." We test it again. Once it's reliable, we continue building.

By the end of class, at least ten expectations have been set, tested, and reinforced. The students leave sharper, more focused, and more confident than when they arrived. The next class begins with a review of every single brick to make sure nothing has shifted. This is how you build a house that lasts.

Being that kind of architect takes focus. It means you have to remember every brick you've laid and every expectation you've set. When one slips, you need to fix it immediately. The longer you wait, the weaker the house becomes. To keep from missing anything, you need two things: a sharp memory of the expectations you've set and a deep knowledge of the material you are teaching. The more you know your subject, the faster you can spot when an expectation has not been met. The faster you spot it, the easier it is to keep the student engaged.

This matters now more than ever. Technology has shortened attention spans, especially in young people. If you are slow to correct missed expectations, you lose their focus. Your house weakens, and their engagement disappears. That's why your goal is to become a world-class architect who can build quickly without cutting corners. This doesn't mean you skip steps or rush ahead. It means you provide feedback at the right time and add new expectations as soon as the student is ready for them.

Here's an example from one of my martial arts classes. After making a connection with my students, I set the first expectation: move fast and respond with a loud "yes, sir" when I ask them to sit down or stand up. Once they showed they could do this on their own, I moved them from the Test phase to the Notice phase. Then I added another expectation: respond the same way when I ask them to line up. Once they caught on, they advanced again.

The next expectation was performing their kicking combination without error. As they tried, I noticed some mistakes. I quickly addressed the mistakes and asked if they understood. But here's where it got interesting. Many of the students responded slowly and without the loud "yes, sir." This was the moment to reset an earlier expectation. If I let it slide, I would have weakened everything we'd built. So I stopped and reminded them of the standard. Quick, strong, loud. I didn't move forward until they did it right.

This is what separates an average instructor from a world-class instructor. Average instructors let little things slip. World-class instructors address them immediately. These students weren't ready for the Observe phase yet because they hadn't proven mastery. Resetting the expectation kept them in the Test phase where they needed to be.

Once they fixed the response and corrected the kicking errors, we resumed practicing the combination. Now they were ready to move toward the Observe phase again. My focus at that point was on catching them doing it right and praising them for correcting their mistakes. Once I saw them succeed multiple times, I filed that expectation into my long-term memory. In my mind, they had earned the Test phase for the kicking combination. The next time I asked them to perform it, I would start them in the Test phase with hopes of moving them back to Observe.

At that point, I had a choice. I could stack another expectation on top of the kicking combination or move to a different one. The decision depends on the group. Younger students under age seven often struggle with extra layers of complexity. Older students can usually handle more. But every student is different. I've had six-year-olds who could manage more complexity than some twelve-year-olds. You have to know your students.

If I feel they can handle more, I might add the expectation that every kick must show a fully bent knee before extending. During the Notice phase, I would watch closely, looking for opportunities to praise those who met this expectation. Once the whole group performed it well, I would repeat the process and add another expectation that fits their ability and matches the day's goal.

This cycle repeats itself all class long. Sit down, line up, take a knee—every time I see a missed expectation, I reset it until they prove they've earned the Observe phase. Students may move back and forth between Test and Observe for a while, but the goal is always the same: get them to Remind.

Now that you've seen how the MENTOR Method works step by step, it's time to look at how it plays out in practice. The framework gives you the tools, but the real value comes when you see it applied in real teaching and coaching situations. In the next section, we'll walk through practical examples—including how legendary coach John Wooden used these same principles to build one of the most successful programs in sports history.

Takeaways

- Each expectation is like a brick — carefully placed, revisited, and strengthened over time.

- Small slips weaken the structure, so correct missed expectations immediately.

- Never move forward until the foundation is solid — average instructors let things slide, world-class instructors reset the standard.

- Match the complexity of expectations to the age and ability of your students.

- The goal is to get the students to the Remind phase.

PART 8

PRACTICAL TOOLS AND APPLICATION

You now understand the framework of the MENTOR Method and the mindset behind it. But knowing the framework is not enough—you need tools you can actually use in real time while teaching. That's what this section is for.

The following chapters take the principles we've covered and put them into practice. Think of this as your toolbox. Each tool is designed to help you in specific situations: setting expectations, giving feedback, keeping students engaged, and handling challenges when they come.

Some of these tools will feel natural to you right away. Others may feel awkward at first. That's normal. Just like learning a new kick, technique, or sequence, the more you practice these tools, the smoother they will become.

The key is not to try to use them all at once. Start with one or two, practice them until they feel natural, then add more. Over time, you'll develop your own rhythm and know which tool to pull out for each moment.

Remember, tools are only as good as the person using them. If you use them without presence, clarity, or consistency, they will lose their power. But if you apply them with confidence, care, and respect, these tools will transform your teaching.

- How to use your voice and communication skills as your strongest tool.

- How to set up drills and directions that maximize learning.

- How to give praise and feedback that actually sticks.

- How to address behavior without losing control or respect.

- How to keep parents engaged and on your side.

By the end, you'll have a set of practical strategies you can rely on in any situation. These tools will help you not only manage your class but also lead it with authority, care, and effectiveness.

———

PART 8A

COMMUNICATION TOOLS

As instructors, our voice is the most powerful tool we have. Long before students notice how sharp our kicks are or how smooth our forms look, they notice how we speak. Our tone, our choice of words, and our ability to capture attention can either build trust and excitement or cause students to disengage.

Strong communication happens when every point has meaning. Every direction, correction, or encouragement we give is a chance to either strengthen or weaken the connection with our students. The best instructors use their voice like a craftsman uses a tool—clear, precise, and intentional.

In this section, you'll learn practical ways to use your voice and words to:

- Give clear and simple instructions that students actually remember

- Hold attention and keep energy high in both small and large groups

- Use analogies and storytelling to make concepts click faster

- Commentate with energy and variety so students stay engaged

- Develop a tone and rhythm that builds confidence and respect

Communication connects your knowledge to your students' growth. Mastering your voice and communication skills will make you not only a better instructor, but also a leader your students want to follow.

BECOME A BLACK BELT COMMUNICATOR

Did you know that only a small part of communication comes from the words you use? Studies show that about 7% is words, 38% is tone of voice, and 55% is body language.

That means what you say actually matters far less than how you say it. As instructors, this truth changes everything. If you want to lead effectively, inspire effort, and keep your students engaged, you must strive to become a black belt in communication.

A black belt communicator doesn't just give directions. They speak in a way that captures attention, moves students to action, and builds trust. They use their voice, tone, pacing, and presence to make every word count.

Think about it: how often do we assume that because we said something, our students heard it? In reality, many times they didn't. The disconnect came from our delivery, not their ability to listen.

As leaders, our goal is to communicate so clearly and so powerfully that students:

- Look up and lean in when we speak.

- Feel our passion and want to match it with effort.

- Stay motivated to push themselves further.

- Trust our guidance enough to follow it without hesitation.

When you communicate at this level, students won't just hear your words — they'll feel them. They'll be more focused, more connected, and more willing to give their best effort.

So, as we step into this section, commit to sharpening your communication just as you would sharpen a technique. Don't settle for being "good enough." Work to master your voice, your tone, and your presence. Because when you do, you'll be leaving an imprint that stays with them long after they move on.

This is what it means to be a black belt communicator.

Key Reminder

Students may forget the exact words you used, but they will never forget how your presence, tone, and body language made them feel. Speak with clarity, passion, and confidence: every class, every time.

ASK DON'T TELL

Whether you are a teacher, instructor, coach, boss, or parent, the natural instinct when giving an expectation or feedback is to simply state it. But there's a more effective approach: turn it into a question.

Asking instead of telling forces the student to think for themselves. When the brain struggles to find an answer, the learning sticks deeper. Rather than being a barrier, struggle can be a vital step to mastery.

This approach also taps into human nature. We all care more about our own ideas than those of others. When a student feels like they created the idea or discovered the answer on their own, they own it. And when you own something, you pay closer attention to it. Asking instead of telling gives the student ownership of the learning process.

It also keeps engagement high. When you're the only one talking in statements, the student's brain goes idle. But when you ask questions, you pull them back into the process. Their mind stay active, alert, and connected to the lesson.

The temptation is to always jump in and tell because it feels faster. It's the same as saying, "I'll just do it myself. It'ss quicker." That may seem true at the moment, but the cost is high. If you always give the answer, the student will always depend on you. They'll look to you for every solution instead of developing independence. And remember: the ultimate goal is for the student to perform the skill or understand the concept without your help.

This doesn't mean you run your class or session entirely on questions. Guidance still matters. At times, you will need to provide direct answers or corrections. But the key is balance. Let the student wrestle with the question first. Allow them to experience that productive struggle, and only step in with feedback once they've tried.

Think of it like planting a seed. If you do all the work for the seed—dig the hole, add the water, give it sunlight, and even try to force it open—it never grows strong. But when you let the seed struggle against the soil on its own, it develops roots that last. The same is true for your students. Asking instead of telling gives them the space to grow strong roots.

There are no shortcuts in learning. Shortcuts only create detours that delay mastery. Asking instead of telling may feel slower at first, but it builds long-term independence, confidence, and ownership of learning.

And here's the bigger picture: asking instead of telling lays the foundation for addressing behavior, which we will explore in the next chapter.

Examples

Martial arts class

Instead of saying: "Bend your knee more on that kick."

Ask: "Did you feel your knee bend before you kicked, or did it stay straight?"

Classroom

Instead of saying: "That's the wrong answer."

Ask: "Walk me through how you got to that answer—what step did you take first?"

Soccer field

Instead of saying: "Pass with the inside of your foot."

Ask: "Which part of your foot will give you the most control for this pass?"

Parenting at home

Instead of saying: "You forgot to put your dish away."

Ask: "Where do your dishes go after dinner?"

Takeaways

- Asking instead of telling makes learning stick because it forces the student to think.

- It keeps engagement high—questions activate the brain, statements often shut it down.

- Ownership of the idea increases motivation and attention.

- Telling feels faster but creates long-term dependence.

- Balance is key—ask first, then guide with feedback if needed.

- Use questions across all settings: martial arts, school, sports, and home.

- Asking instead of telling is the foundation for addressing behavior effectively.

When we speak to our class, whether giving directions, teaching a skill, or providing feedback, we must always remember that students only have a short window of attention. Today, people are used to information coming fast. Think about short videos online: if they don't grab attention in seconds, people scroll. Students are no different. If we talk too long or clutter our words, we lose them. That's why our goal as instructors is to keep communication clear and simple.

Why Simplicity Matters

Every sentence should have purpose. The more extra words we add, the more likely the real message gets buried. One of the biggest distractions is filler words—empty sounds we use when we're thinking. Instead of fearing silence, we need to use it. Pauses are powerful. They give students time to think and process what we say. A short pause between sentences is like a period on a page—it shows the thought is complete and keeps the message sharp.

The Power of Practice

The key is practice. You won't remove filler words just by knowing about them. You must train yourself to speak in short, simple sentences. Record yourself. Get feedback from another instructor. Pay attention to how often you add fillers. The more you practice, the stronger and more confident your words will sound.

Clear vs. Unclear Directions

Here are some examples of what this looks like in real class situations:

Unclear: "Okay guys, what I'd like for everyone to do now is get into a line somewhere over there so we can get ready for the next drill, alright?"

Clear: "Line up on the black line next to Mr. Smith."

Unclear: "Um, I think what we're going to do now is maybe try some kicks with a partner, so grab a paddle if you want, and find someone about your size."

Clear: "Find a partner of your size. Each pair grabs one paddle. Stand on this line facing each other."

Unclear: "Alright, I mean, let's just try harder, you know?"

Clear: "Everyone—give me your best effort this round. Ready? Go."

Short, direct sentences get the class moving faster, reduce confusion, and keep engagement high.

Cheat Sheet: Replacing Filler Words

Common Filler Words to Avoid

- um

- uh

- you know

- like

- so

- okay (when overused as a crutch)

- basically

- alright

- kind of / sort of

- I mean

Stronger Replacements

- Pause – instead of filling the space, let silence work for you.

- Direct action words – "Line up," "Begin," "Switch," "Stop."

- Confirmation words – "Yes," "Correct," "Exactly."

- Transition words – "Next," "Now," "Here's the focus."

- Simple emphasis – "Listen," "Focus," "Pay attention."

Practice Tips

- Record yourself teaching and count how many filler words you use.

- Replace every filler word with either silence or one strong word.

- Rehearse instructions in advance using only the clearest, simplest words.

- Ask a colleague or assistant to give you hand signals whenever you slip into fillers.

Takeaway

The clearer and simpler your words, the stronger your impact. Speak less, say more, and let silence be part of your teaching.

USING WORDS TO GET THE BEST OUT OF YOUR STUDENTS

The words you choose—and how you say them—can either unlock a student's best effort or shut them down completely. Teaching is not just about transferring knowledge; it's about pulling out what's inside the student. Your words are the tool that makes this happen.

Tone Over Volume

Authority does not come from yelling. In fact, yelling often communicates frustration, which weakens your influence. A calm, confident tone is far more powerful. The student hears not just what you say but how you say it. If your tone is steady and controlled, the student feels safe and respects your authority.

Positive Framing

Always frame your words in the direction you want the student to go. Instead of saying, "Don't be lazy with that kick," say, "Show me your strongest kick." Both address the same issue, but one motivates while the other discourages. Positive framing turns correction into encouragement.

Keep It Short

As I mentioned earlier, less is more. Long lectures kill engagement. Students, especially children, stop listening after a few seconds of rambling. Say what you need to say in as few words as possible. Direct, clear words carry the most power.

Tie Praise to Expectation

When a student meets an expectation, use words of praise that connect directly to the behavior. Instead of saying, "Good job," say, "Great job snapping that kick right when I said 'go.'" This way, the student knows exactly what they did right, and others in the group know the standard..

Questions Over Commands

Asking questions instead of always telling keeps engagement high. A command tells the student what to do. A question forces them to think, struggle, and own the answer. "Should you be standing tall or slouching right now?" is far more effective than "Stop slouching." Questions lead to ownership, and ownership leads to mastery.

Match Words With Body Language

Your words lose their power if your face and body don't match them. Saying, "Good job" with a blank stare or crossed arms sends the wrong message. Your facial expressions, posture, and gestures should always support your words. Energy, warmth, and confidence are communicated just as much through your body as through your voice.

The Big Picture

Words carry weight and shape how people think and choose.They can build confidence, spark motivation, and guide students toward mastery. They can also discourage, frustrate, or shut down effort if used carelessly. When you keep your tone calm, your phrases positive, your words short, and your questions sharp, you set the stage for your students to give their best.

When you learn to use words in this way, you stop just teaching—you start drawing the very best out of every student.

Takeaways

- Use tone, not volume, to show authority.

- Frame words in the positive direction.

- Keep your words short and clear.

- Tie praise directly to the expectation met.

- Ask more than you tell to spark thinking.

- Match your body language with your words.

THE COUNTING VOICE

When you count in class, your voice is not just keeping time — it is setting the tone for the entire room. A strong counting voice communicates confidence, clarity, and energy. If your voice is weak or flat, students will lose focus. If your voice is sharp, quick, and to the point, students will snap to attention and stay engaged.

Think of your counting voice like a drumbeat. It should be crisp, consistent, and easy to follow. Each number should almost jolt the students like a quick shake of energy. One. Two. Three. Four. Clear, firm, and direct.

But not every group of students will need the same delivery. Sometimes you'll need to bring the intensity high to energize a large class. Other times, especially with shy or younger students, you may need to soften your tone to avoid overwhelming them. What should always stay the same is the clarity and confidence behind your count.

The Three Stages of Counting

There are three main ways to count when practicing or teaching a sequence—whether it's a combination, a drill, or a form. Each stage gradually increases the level of difficulty and responsibility for the student. The end goal is always to move them from relying on you to performing independently.

Stage One: Giving the Answers

The first way of counting is simply calling out the exact technique.

For example: "Low block, punch. Low block, punch. Low block, punch."

This stage makes it easiest for students to follow along because you are essentially giving them the answers. It's useful for beginners or when introducing a new sequence. But remember—it is also the least beneficial for long-term retention, since students don't have to think much for themselves.

Stage Two: Generalized Cues

The second stage makes the process a little more abstract. Instead of naming the exact technique, you call out broader categories.

- Instead of "inside block," say "block."

- Instead of "punch," say "strike."

Now the student has to think: Which block? Which strike? You are still guiding them, but they must take a step toward independence.

Stage Three: No Hints

The third stage removes hints altogether. At this level, you simply count or give neutral prompts:

- "One, two, three."

- "Next, next, next."

This forces students to use their memory and critical thinking to recall what comes next without depending on your words. It's the most challenging form of counting—and also the most beneficial for long-term mastery.

Progression and Judgement

As an instructor, your job is to use good judgment on when to progress to the next stage. Beginners may need Stage One for a while, but if you stay there too long, they will become dependent on you. The ultimate win is when a student can run through the entire sequence from beginning to end with nothing more than your simple counting.

Keys to a Strong Counting Voice

- Quick and Sharp – Don't drag out the numbers. Keep them short and direct.

- Penetrating – Each count should be strong enough that students can't help but snap to the movement.

- Consistent Rhythm – Maintain a steady tempo so students feel the flow of the sequence.

- Adjustable Energy – Raise or lower intensity depending on the age, size, and personality of the group.

Example

Instead of a flat, lifeless count like: "One... two... three... four..."

Deliver it with energy and punch: "One! Two! Three! Four!"

Students should feel the difference immediately in their effort and focus.

Takeaway

Start by giving the answers, move to general hints, and finish by removing hints completely. This progression trains students not only to remember the sequence but also to think for themselves and build confidence in their ability to perform independently.

Keep in mind that your counting voice is one of your most important teaching tools. When used correctly, it keeps students in rhythm, keeps their energy high, and shows them that you are fully engaged. Strong counts lead to strong effort.

DELIVERING DIRECTIONS

If you want your drills and classes to run smoothly, you must learn how to deliver directions effectively. Clear directions remove confusion, save time, and keep your students engaged.

Be Close Enough to Be Heard

Always make sure you are standing close enough to your students. In a large training area, or when other classes are happening at the same time, students may not hear you if you stay too far away. If they can't hear, they can't succeed. Either bring students closer to you or walk around as you explain.

Control Your Volume and Pace

Your voice should be loud enough for everyone in your group to hear, but not so loud that you distract other classes. Speak slowly, especially during the most important parts of the directions. If you rush, your words will be missed. Stretch out key words and enunciate clearly so the important parts land.

Use Demonstrations

A demonstration is often more powerful than an explanation. Ask a star student or assistant to show what you are describing. This frees you to watch the group and confirm they are paying attention. It also provides a live example for visual learners.

Hold Students Accountable

If you notice students drifting, call on one of them to repeat or demonstrate what you just explained. A surprise pop quiz moment keeps everyone alert and listening. When you do this, keep it respectful and quick— never embarrassing.

Summarize the Key Points

After explaining, follow up with a summary of the key actions. For example:

"Line up on the black and gray line. Right foot forward. One front snap kick, then go to the end of the line."

Short, clear, and complete.

Random Demonstrations

Don't be afraid to ask a random student to show the directions before the drill starts. This accomplishes two things: it lets you check if the class understands, and it keeps every student engaged since they know they could be chosen.

Practice for Precision

Like any skill, delivering directions improves with practice. Challenge yourself to keep your instructions quick, clear, and efficient. The more precise you are, the smoother your class will run.

Key Reminders

- Be close enough to be heard.

- Adjust volume so your group hears you without disturbing others.

- Speak slowly and enunciate key points.

- Use student demonstrations to reinforce.

- Hold students accountable with quick checks.

- Summarize the essentials in one sentence.

- Randomly choose students to confirm understanding.

- Always aim for short, clear, and efficient instructions.

GIVING PRODUCTIVE FEEDBACK

When giving feedback to students, you must always make it specific, clear, and useful. Vague words like "that one," "over there," or "thing" don't help the student know what to fix. Instead, use exact words: "Move your left foot forward," or "Turn your shoulders toward the flag." This removes confusion and shows the student exactly what success looks like.

There are two main types of feedback words: **redirecting** and **reinforcing**.

- **Redirecting words** are used when a student does not perform something correctly. They help steer the student back on track. Examples: "Nope," "Not yet," "Almost," followed by a clear correction. For instance: "Almost—bring your hand higher to your collarbone. Yes, now that's it."

- **Reinforcing words** are used when a student performs something correctly. They build confidence and let the student know they're on the right path. Examples: "Yes," "Correct," "That's it," "Exactly." The key is to deliver these with **energy and authenticity**. A flat "good job" sounds fake, but an energetic "Yes! That's exactly how it's done" motivates the student to repeat that effort.

Balance both types. Too much redirecting without reinforcement can discourage a student. Too much praise without corrections leaves them stuck at the same level. The art is in **using both with the right tone, timing, and balance**.

Also, adjust your delivery by age and maturity. Younger students need more energy and encouragement. Older or more advanced students need feedback that respects their maturity—straightforward and to the point, without sounding childish or condescending.

Cheat Sheet: Redirecting vs. Reinforcing

Redirecting Words (to correct)

- Nope
- Not yet
- Almost
- Try again
- Bring it higher/lower/sharper

Reinforcing Words (to confirm)

- Yes
- Correct
- Exactly
- That's it
- Perfect

Keys to Remember

- Always follow redirecting words with an explicit instruction.

- Deliver reinforcing words with energy and authenticity.

- Match your tone to the age and maturity of the student.

- Aim for balance—too much of one without the other is ineffective.

Sample Dialogue

Instructor: "Nope, not yet—your front foot is too far back. Step it forward one mat length. Yes, stop, perfect."

Student: (adjusts stance)

Instructor: "Yes! That's the strong stance I want to see."

Instructor: "Almost—your hand is halfway. Bring it up to your collarbone. Good, now press it tight. Perfect!"

Instructor: "That roundhouse kick had great power, but you leaned back too much. Try it again. Yes, that one—exactly how it should look. Keep repeating it like that."

This back-and-forth shows how quickly redirecting words plus clear instructions guide the student, while reinforcing words and energy make them eager to repeat the correct behavior.

THE PROGRESSION OF CORRECTION

When providing feedback to your students, it's important to have a method. If you correct too much too quickly, you risk overwhelming the student. If you correct too little, you risk them staying stuck. The solution is to use a progression of correction. Start broad and simple, then layer in details as the student grows.

Start Simple

Always begin with the big picture. For example, if you are teaching a front kick, your first correction might be, *"Lift your knee higher."*

This gives the student a clear and easy target without overloading them. At this stage, they don't need to worry about every small detail. They just need to get comfortable and build confidence.

Narrow the Focus

Once the student has practiced the broader correction, you can narrow it down: *"Point your toes back before you kick."*

Now they are still working on the front kick, but with more detail. This keeps their progress moving forward while still being manageable.

Add the Details

As they improve, you can layer in even smaller corrections: *"Snap your foot out a little faster at the top of the kick."*

Notice that this is not where you start. Instead, you save this for later once the student is ready.

One or Two Corrections at a Time

Students can only process so much at once. Never pile on ten things for them to fix. Instead:

- Give one or two corrections.

- Let them practice.

- Reassess and then add another layer if they're ready.

Know the Student

The level of correction depends on the student in front of you. Ask yourself:

- What is their maturity level?

- Are they engaged or distracted?

- Are they giving effort or just going through the motions?

- What stage of mastery are they at? (beginner, intermediate, advanced)

- How much time do I have in this drill or class?

The answers will help you decide how much correction to give and how detailed to make it.

Watch for Engagement

Even if your corrections are right, they won't matter if the student is losing interest. Keep an eye out:

- Are they looking frustrated?

- Do they seem bored or irritated?

- Are they disengaging because of too much feedback?

If so, scale back or move on. Your goal is progress, not perfection in one class.

Key Takeaways

The progression of correction is simple:

1. Start broad – big picture, easy focus.

2. Narrow in – one or two targeted corrections.

3. Add details – only when the student is ready.

By following this progression, you'll keep your students engaged, motivated, and improving step by step.

GIVING FEEDBACK TO ADULT STUDENTS

Teaching adults is not the same as teaching children. Adults process feedback differently, and the way you speak to them can make or break their experience in your class. They notice the details — your words, tone, and even body language — so your approach must be intentional.

Know the Student

Before you can give effective feedback, you need to understand why the adult is here. Are they looking for fitness? Do they want to learn the art? Are they motivated by stress relief or self-defense? Knowing their goals shapes how you coach them.

You also want to be aware of their personality. Are they confident and prideful? Or are they more hesitant and insecure? The way you frame feedback should adjust to who is in front of you.

Be Humbly Confident

Adult students will not respect feedback if they feel you lack knowledge or certainty. At the same time, they will shut down if you come across as arrogant or condescending. The key is humble confidence — knowing your material well, speaking clearly, and delivering corrections with respect.

When you present yourself this way, adults recognize that you are skilled and trustworthy, but not overbearing.

Stay Alert and Attentive

Adults are very aware of whether or not you are paying attention. If you seem distracted, they will notice immediately. Watch closely, stay present, and respond quickly to what you see. This builds trust and keeps them engaged.

Make It Conversational, Not Commanding

Children often respond well to short, direct commands. Adults usually prefer feedback that feels like collaboration. Instead of saying, *"Fix your wrist,"* try:

- "Could you rotate your wrist a little bit inwards?"

- "Try shifting your stance slightly wider."

This conversational tone makes adults feel respected, not ordered around. It also opens the door for them to process the feedback and own the adjustment.

Review and Apply

When giving feedback to adults, always keep these points in mind:

- Establish connection – get to know their goals and personality.

- Be humbly confident – clear, knowledgeable, but never arrogant.

- Stay attentive – adults will notice if you aren't paying attention.

- Make it conversational – phrase feedback as guidance, not commands.

When you apply these principles, you'll earn the respect of your adult students while helping them improve. More importantly, you'll create an environment where they feel valued, motivated, and eager to return.

Using Analogies to Increase Comprehension

One of the most powerful tools an instructor can use is the analogy. An analogy takes something unfamiliar and compares it to something a student already understands. When used correctly, it can turn confusion into clarity in a matter of seconds.

Think about how often students struggle when you tell them directly what to do. They hear the words, but the concept doesn't click. Analogies shift their perspective. By linking a new skill to a familiar image or idea, you open a door in their mind that helps the lesson land.

1. Match the Analogy to the Student

Not all analogies work for all ages. A four-year-old won't understand if you compare a stance to the foundation of a skyscraper, but they might understand if you tell them it's like being a tree with roots in the ground. On the other hand, a teenager may find the tree analogy too childish, but they'll connect with the skyscraper comparison. Always measure your analogy against the maturity, age, and background of the student in front of you.

2. Keep It Short and Sharp

The power of an analogy comes from its simplicity. The moment you start over-explaining, the impact is lost. Think of it as a quick spark to ignite understanding, not a full lecture. For example, instead of spending three minutes describing balance, you could say, "Balance is like riding a bike—if you lean too far, you fall." That single sentence paints the picture and allows the student to immediately adjust.

3. Know When to Abandon It

Not every analogy will hit. Sometimes you'll see blank stares, and that's your cue to move on. Forcing an analogy only creates more confusion. Be willing to switch quickly to another example or drop it entirely and return to basics.

4. Don't Overuse Them

Analogies are a tool, not the entire toolbox. If you fill your class with analogy after analogy, students will get confused, and the lesson will lose focus. Use them sparingly, only when you see a student struggling to grasp the concept directly.

5. Examples in Action

- Teaching a punch: "It's like throwing a ball—your shoulder, elbow, and wrist all work together."

- Teaching focus: "Imagine your eyes are like a flashlight. Wherever the light shines, that's where your attention goes."

- Teaching effort: "Your energy is like a battery—if you give half effort, you only give half your power."

These simple pictures stick in students' minds long after the class is over.

Go-To Analogies for Martial Arts Instruction

Balance

- Like standing on a surfboard—if you lean too far, you'll fall.

- Like being a tree—your roots keep you steady, but your branches can move.

Focus

- Your eyes are like a flashlight—where the beam points is where your mind goes.

- Like aiming a camera—if it's blurry, the picture isn't clear.

Speed

- Like snapping a towel—fast, sharp, and sudden.

- Like lightning—quick, powerful, and done before you know it.

Power

- Like swinging a hammer—the strength comes from your whole body, not just your arm.

- Like a whip—loose, then explosive at the end.

Discipline

- Like brushing your teeth—you do it every day, even if you don't feel like it.

- Like building with blocks—one step at a time makes something strong.

Effort

- Like a battery—if you give half effort, you only use half your power.

- Like blowing up a balloon—if you stop halfway, it never takes full shape.

Teamwork

- Like rowing a boat—if only one person rows, you go in circles.

- Like playing music in a band—everyone has to stay on rhythm.

Key Takeaway

When used wisely, analogies transform teaching. They take difficult concepts and make them simple, engaging, and memorable. The key is to choose the right analogy for the right student, keep it short, and use it sparingly. Done well, your students won't just understand the skill—they'll feel it.

One of the most powerful tools you have as an instructor is your voice. The way you use your words can transform the energy of the entire class. When you become a dynamic commentator, you are not just teaching—you are narrating, energizing, and directing the room in real time.

Think of a sports commentator. They don't just say what is happening. They describe it with energy and excitement so the audience stays engaged. As an instructor, your students are your audience, but they are also the players. Your commentary helps them know what matters, where to focus, and how to push themselves further.

Here's what it looks like in action. As soon as you see a student doing something well, you call it out for the whole group to hear. "Yes! Sarah snapped her kick with power. That's exactly how it should look." This does three things at once. It praises the student who did it right, it shows the rest of the class the standard to aim for, and it lifts the energy of the room.

Dynamic commentary also works with effort, not just results. If a student is giving maximum effort, you let the group know: "Look at James hustling to the line. That's the speed I want to see." By pointing it out, you reward the effort publicly, which makes the rest of the group want to match it.

You can also use dynamic commentary to build friendly competition between students or groups. Divide the class and keep a running dialogue of who's winning. "Team One's stances are looking sharp—Team Two, are you going to let them take it?" or "Ava's focus is locked in—who's going to catch her?" This creates excitement without negativity. It gives students a reason to push harder and celebrate each other's efforts.

Your commentary doesn't always have to be positive. If the group's energy drops, you can also use it to call them back up: "That response was too quiet. I know you can be louder." This keeps expectations clear while still engaging everyone.

The key is to keep your words short, sharp, and filled with energy. Long lectures will slow the class down and cause students to lose attention. But quick bursts of commentary keep the pace moving and keep students listening.

When you commentate, you are doing more than just talking—you are shaping the atmosphere of the room. You are telling the students through your words what is important, what is worth repeating, and what must be corrected. The louder, clearer, and more specific your commentary is, the faster students will learn.

Takeaways

- Commentary keeps energy high and attention sharp.

- Praise and correction become more powerful when spoken out loud to the group.

- Call out effort, not just results.

- Use commentary to build friendly competition that drives motivation and teamwork.

- Keep your words short, specific, and filled with energy.

- A dynamic commentator directs both the focus and the atmosphere of the room.

PART 8B

PRAISE & MOTIVATION TOOLS

It All Comes Down to Praise

Children are created to yearn for praise. Praise acts as their compass, showing them what is right and what is wrong. It is what builds their foundation of personal security—especially when it comes from a trusted adult with whom they have a strong connection.

In reality, all people seek praise in some form. A child looks for it from their parents or teacher. A spouse looks for it from their partner. An employee looks for it from their manager. Many even seek it from strangers, which is why posting selfies on social media has become so addictive. Praise is wired into us.

As an instructor, you must keep this truth front and center in your mind. It should always be your ultimate goal for the student: for them to earn your praise. The keyword here is **earn**. Praise is only valuable when it is earned, and even very young children can sense when it is not. Empty praise feels fake and loses its power.

Praise is earned when an expectation has been met. That's why it is so important to clearly communicate the expectation and make sure the student understands it. Once that is in place, your role is to watch closely. If you sense the student will not be able to meet the expectation, adjust it quickly so they can succeed.

The goal is for the student to experience earned praise as early as possible in the lesson. When this happens, it builds momentum. They want more. But if you wait too long, their motivation and engagement drop quickly. That's why you must set expectations in a way that allows them to earn praise quickly and fairly.

Be careful not to make it too easy. If the challenge is too small, the praise feels hollow. Students may even feel like you are trying to trick them. On the other hand, if the challenge is too big, they will fail, and no praise will come. The art of teaching is finding the sweet spot where the expectation is achievable but still stretches the student.

As the lesson continues, you gradually increase the difficulty of earning praise. Each step should connect back to your objective for the day. The student continues to seek your praise, and each time they earn it, their confidence, motivation, and engagement grow.

Positional Authority Isn't Enough

Positional authority—your uniform, title, or role—may give you a platform, but it is not enough for students to want your praise. For praise to matter, you must build a connection where the student genuinely cares what you think about them and wants to earn your approval. When this connection exists, your praise carries real weight. Without it, your words risk sounding empty, no matter how loud or clear they are.

Why Praise Matters

Every student longs to feel noticed and valued. Praise gives them that recognition. It builds confidence, deepens trust, and motivates them to keep trying. But praise only works when it is genuine, earned, and specific. False praise—telling a student they did something well when they didn't—damages trust and weakens your influence.

Instead, set up small, clear opportunities for students to succeed so that your praise is always honest. For example, even if a student cannot yet kick very high, you can sincerely praise their effort or focus without pretending their kick was perfect.

Rules of Praise

- Praise quickly — the sooner it follows the action, the stronger the connection.

- Be specific — always tie the praise to the exact expectation that was met.

- Make it earned — never give praise for half effort or unfinished work.

- Use group praise strategically — praising one student motivates the rest.

- Turn it into a challenge — after praising, ask the group, "Who else can do this?" or "Who can do better?"

- Raise the standard gradually — make praise harder to earn as the lesson continues.

Earned praise is the most powerful tool you have. It fuels confidence, drives engagement, and helps students build the discipline to keep growing.

WAYS OF GIVING PRAISE

Conversational Praise

Conversational praise is when you stop and directly acknowledge a student, either privately or publicly.

- Private Praise: One-on-one, short, and heartfelt. Make eye contact. Keep your words simple and specific. Instead of "Good job," say, "Great job turning your foot exactly the way I showed you." Use a pitch that sounds sincere—too high sounds fake, too low sounds unenthusiastic.

- Public Praise: Highlight a student in front of the group. This could include a high five or a short round of applause, but use these sparingly. Public praise is powerful because it reinforces behavior for everyone: "Look at how Alex is standing at attention—that's exactly the focus I want to see." Other students will quickly adjust because they want that same recognition.

Feedback Praise

Feedback praise is different. It's short, energetic, and tied to an immediate action the student just performed. This is when your tone and body language carry the most weight.

- Use strong one- or two-word phrases: "Yes!" "Great!" "Perfect!"

- Match your body language with your words—lean in, point with an open hand, or nod with energy.

- Keep it quick. Feedback praise should feel like a spark of energy that reinforces the correct action right away.

For example, if a student finally performs a low block correctly after several tries, don't just say, "There you go." Instead, lean in with energy: "Yes! That's exactly how you do it!"

Group Praise and Competition

Praise is also very powerful when you are teaching more than one student. Once you praise one student in front of the group, the rest of the group will want to earn praise too. This becomes your main strategy to encourage more students to meet the expectation—and even go beyond it. Friendly competition is a powerful way to increase motivation and engagement.

When you do this, make sure you clearly communicate out loud what the student did correctly so the whole group can hear it. Then add the cherry on top: ask, "Who else can do what this student just did?" or "Who can do better?" This simple move creates instant drive for the rest of the group to rise to the challenge.

Key Reminder

Praise works best when it's earned, specific, and genuine. Use conversational praise to build connection, and feedback praise to reinforce action. Both should be delivered with energy, eye contact, and sincerity.

The Do's and Don'ts of Giving Praise

Do's

- Be specific: Praise the exact action ("Great job snapping your kick back").

- Make eye contact: Show the student you mean it.

- Keep it short: One or two sentences at most.

- Use the right tone: Energetic but genuine, not fake or flat.

- Balance: Mix redirecting feedback with reinforcing praise.

Don'ts

- Don't praise what isn't earned—it breaks trust.

- Don't overuse high fives or applause—they lose impact.

- Don't be vague: Avoid "Good job" without context.

- Don't use the wrong pitch—too high sounds fake, too low sounds negative.

- Don't forget body language: Praise without energy feels empty.

The Truth About Motivation

Since our goal is to retain our students in the long term, we need to review their sources of motivation.

The first is **entertainment**. Students who first begin their journey with us are motivated to come back to class because it's new, fun, and exciting. Entertainment is always a factor to pay attention to if we want to keep students engaged and motivated. We should always be asking: are our classes fun? Are they exciting? Are we, as instructors, enjoyable to be around? While entertainment should not be our only focus, it is often the first motivator that gets students to return.

The second is **obeying authority**. Every student—whether they show it openly or not—wants someone to coach them, hold them accountable, and care about them. A strong authority figure provides guidance and direction that many students crave, even if they don't admit it.

The third is **social advancement**. Students want to feel connected to others in the class and, even more, feel like they are advancing in those relationships and compared to their peers. Some students will be motivated more by this than others, but the desire to connect and advance socially is built into all of us.

The fourth is **self-achievement**. Students want to feel like they are improving, earning, or growing. This could be getting a new stripe, earning a belt, learning a new technique, or improving on a skill they've been practicing for months. That inner sense of progress is very powerful.

Now let's look at how these motivators show up at different ages:

- **Ages 4–6**: Motivation comes mostly from entertainment and obeying authority. At this age, they are not yet driven by self-achievement or social advancement. The classes must be fun, exciting, and structured by a leader they respect.

- **Ages 7–9**: Motivation expands to entertainment, social advancement, and obeying authority. Students at this stage start to care about social connections, relationships, and friendly competition. Partner drills are especially effective here.

- **Ages 10–15**: All four motivators come into play. These students need entertainment, self-achievement, social advancement, and authority. A common myth is that older kids don't like authority. In truth, they crave it even more, as long as it comes from someone they respect and trust. At this age, peer approval and social standing are especially powerful motivators.

- **Ages 16 and up**: Motivation comes mostly from self-achievement and social advancement. These students want to get better, go deeper into technique, and build meaningful relationships with like-minded peers.

The Takeaway

To keep students engaged long-term, you must understand which motivators are most powerful for their age group and use them intentionally. Motivation shifts as students grow, but when you align your teaching to what drives them, you keep their energy, focus, and commitment strong.

DRILL DESIGN & MANAGEMENT TOOLS

THE SCULPTOR METHOD

Have you ever watched a sculptor create a masterpiece from a block of clay? At first, the sculptor doesn't start by carving out perfect eyelids or delicate lines in the hair. Instead, they block out the head, shoulders, and body. Only after the large shape begins to take form do they start refining smaller details. The masterpiece is built layer by layer, moving from broad strokes to fine touches.

This is exactly how we should approach teaching our students. Too many instructors get stuck in the details right from the start. They want perfect stances like precise hand placement and flawless timing before the student even understands the bigger motion. The problem is, when you dive straight into details, you overload the student. They get frustrated. They forget what they were even working on. And worst of all, they lose the joy of progress.

Instead, think like a sculptor. Start with the big shapes. Get the general movement, the turns, the big movements. Once the student has the foundation, then begin to refine. Bit by bit, detail by detail, you help them shape their own masterpiece.

The Principle

- Big first, small later. Focus on the large, important motions before zooming in on tiny corrections.

- Details sprinkled over time. Spread out refinements so students can absorb and apply them without overwhelm.

- Progress before perfection. The student should feel momentum, not stuck in endless correction.

The Contrast

Imagine a beginner working on a side kick. The "detail-first" instructor stops them right away: "Your toes are pointed wrong. Your supporting foot isn't pivoted enough. Your knee chamber is off. Your hand's not in the right spot. Your eyes aren't looking the right direction." That student is drowning in feedback. Instead of feeling progress, they feel failure.

Now, imagine applying the Sculptor Method. You start with the big picture: "Lift your knee. Push your foot out. Bring it back." Once they've got the motion, you add, "Good. Now turn your bottom foot a little more." Later: "Great. Now pull your toes back." Over time, the side kick takes shape. Each correction sticks because it was given at the right time.

The Application

The Sculptor Method works best when you think in layers. Teach one layer, let it settle, then add the next.

Example Sequence: Teaching a Form (Pattern)

1. Layer One: Teach the student the order of the steps — left, right, turn, block, punch. Don't correct stances or hands yet.

2. Layer Two: Once the sequence is memorized, confirm the steps of the hand and foot techniques are correct.

3. Layer Three: Next, refine stances — bend the knees, make the base strong.

4. Layer Four: Finally, add finishing touches — height of kicks, correct foot pivoting, power, rhythm, pace.

By spreading it out, the student succeeds at every stage. They see the form taking shape, like a sculpture emerging from clay.

Example Beyond Martial Arts: Basketball Shooting

Wrong Way (Detail-First Coach)

Coach: "Elbow in! No, more in. Fix your wrist angle. You're not flicking your fingers right. Bend your knees deeper. No, not that much. Look at the rim! No, higher arc!"

Result: The player is paralyzed by corrections. They stop shooting naturally because they're too busy thinking about ten things at once.

Right Way (Sculptor Method Coach)

Coach: "Step one — just focus on getting the ball up to the basket. Forget form for now, just shoot."

(Player shoots and makes contact with the rim.)

Coach: "Good. Now step two — keep your body square to the basket every time."

(Player adjusts and shoots again.)

Coach: "Great. Now step three — try flicking your wrist a little at the end."

(Player refines gradually and starts hitting more shots.)

Result: The player is building confidence and rhythm first. Each new detail is layered once the foundation feels natural. Over time, the shot looks clean and smooth, like a sculpture becoming more defined.

Other Sports and Classroom Examples

- **Baseball:** First, just focus on swinging and hitting the ball. Later, add foot position, hip rotation, and grip.

- **Soccer:** First, kick the ball toward the goal with power. Later, refine placement, accuracy, and spin.

- **Classroom Math:** First, understand the big picture — "fractions mean splitting into equal parts." Later, layer in simplification, denominators, and operations.

- **Writing:** First, write down ideas in sentences. Later, refine grammar, structure, and word choice.

Why This Works

1. **It reduces frustration.** Students feel progress instead of being overwhelmed.

2. **It builds confidence.** Success on the big motions gives them momentum.

3. **It makes lessons stick.** When the student has mastered one layer, the next correction has room to land.

4. **It mirrors real mastery.** Every skill in life is learned from broad to fine.

The Checklist

Before giving feedback, ask yourself three quick questions:

1. Am I focusing on the big picture or a tiny detail?

2. Will this correction help them feel progress right now?

3. Is this the right time to add this layer, or should I wait until the foundation is stronger?

If the answer to #1 is "tiny detail" and #3 is "not yet," hold back. Save that correction for later. You'll keep the student motivated and make the details stick when they're ready.

The Takeaway

Teaching is sculpting. If you obsess over details too early, you'll never give your students the chance to see the masterpiece forming. But if you begin with the big picture and slowly add the right details at the right time, you'll shape students who feel progress, stay engaged, and ultimately achieve mastery.

THE ELEMENTS OF A GREAT DRILL

Every great drill has a purpose. If there's no clear purpose, it's not a drill—it's just entertainment. Drills should be designed to teach the curriculum, sharpen skills, and build focus. That means the very first step in planning is asking yourself: Why am I doing this drill? What skill am I trying to improve?

The second step is setting a clear measurement of success. Students need to know what "winning" looks like. How do they earn your praise? How do they know they did it correctly? This measurement must be specific and communicated to the class before they begin.

For example, if the drill is to kick a paddle, you might say: "You must strike with the top of your foot. If you hit with your toes, I won't count it as correct." That's a measurable standard. Or you could add a competition: "Whoever hits the paddle first after I say 'go' wins." Now there's urgency, motivation, and a clear reason to try hard.

Without these measurements, students, especially younger ones, lose motivation. Children under ten rarely work hard simply to "get better." They work hard to please an authority figure and to earn praise. That's why your drill must give them a clear way to succeed and be recognized.

So the formula for a great drill is simple:

1. Set the objective — define what the drill is for.

2. Define the measurement of success — what does "correct" look like?

3. Communicate both clearly — so every student knows the standard before they start.

Practical Examples

- Martial Arts Class: If students are practicing front kicks, the objective might be "kick with proper chamber and re-chamber." The measurement of success could be "your knee must come back up before you set your foot down." Communicate that standard, then watch closely and praise those who meet it.

- Classroom: If students are working on math problems, the objective could be "complete five problems correctly in five minutes." The measurement of success is simple: accuracy and speed. Share that standard, then let them work. Students now know exactly what earns recognition.

- Soccer Practice: If players are practicing passing, the objective is "use the inside of your foot for every pass." The measurement is whether the ball makes clean contact and stays under control. Communicate that, and the players have a clear way to succeed instead of just kicking the ball around.

- Parenting at Home: If the goal is cleaning a bedroom, the objective might be "every toy off the floor and on the shelf." The measurement of success is simple: "The floor must be clear." Tell your child what earns your praise before they start, then recognize them when they meet it.

When you follow these steps, drills stop being busy work and start becoming powerful teaching tools. Students stay engaged, effort increases, and learning accelerates.

Takeaway

A great drill always has a clear purpose, a clear standard, and clear communication—and those three things make all the difference.

THE FLOOR IS QUICKSAND

As soon as your class begins, I want you to imagine that the mat, or the flooring you are teaching on, suddenly turns into quicksand. If your students stay in the same spot for too long, they start sinking deeper and deeper into that quicksand.

This is the mindset you must carry into every lesson: stillness leads to disengagement. A student who stands in one place too long will lose focus, lose energy, and lose connection with you. Movement is what keeps them alive, engaged, and learning.

That means whatever drill you choose, you must make sure students are consistently moving out of their spot. They should not be stuck in the same square of the floor for long periods of time. At KOMA, the standard is that no student should remain in the same spot for more than five minutes. And the best instructors will have their students moving across different areas of the floor, not just stepping in and out of the same place.

Think of it like circulation in the body. If blood sits in one place too long, it clots. Suppose students stay in one place too long, their engagement clots. But when you keep them moving—forward, back, side to side, across the mats—you keep the energy and attention circulating.

This doesn't mean chaos. The movement is purposeful, tied directly to the drill or expectation you've set. For example, instead of practicing kicks in one spot for ten minutes, have them kick while moving down the line. Instead of standing still while you lecture, have them shift into a new stance, change partners, or move to a new formation.

The mats are always quicksand. The moment class begins, you are in a race against disengagement. The instructors who keep their students moving are the ones who keep their students learning.

Real-World Applications

- Classroom: A teacher who has students sit still for long periods loses their attention. Instead, use strategies like standing up to answer questions, moving to a whiteboard, or switching seats for group work. Movement keeps minds active.

- Sports field: A coach who talks too long on the sideline loses the athletes' focus. By mixing explanation with short drills that involve constant movement, the players stay sharp and engaged.

- At home: A parent who gives long instructions while their child sits still often gets ignored. But when they add movement—"Come here and show me how you'd do it"—the child stays involved and learning continues.

Takeaways

- Imagine your mats are quicksand—stillness sinks engagement.

- No student should stand in the same spot for more than five minutes.

- Keep students moving with purpose across the space.

- Movement keeps energy high, focus sharp, and learning active.

NEVER SHOW YOUR CARDS TOO EARLY

With younger students, you must be careful not to move too quickly through drills or material. If you do, engagement can drop fast. The secret is to stretch each part of the drill, concept, or skill for as long as possible—without losing focus—while still aiming at the objective for the day.

The end goal is always the same: transfer the skill or knowledge so the student can achieve mastery. But with younger students, you have only a short window before their attention fades. There is only so much detail you can cover before interest starts to slip.

On the flip side, many instructors make the opposite mistake. They move on too soon—before the student has truly learned anything or before there's any sign of disengagement. This wastes valuable teaching time.

It works just like a card game—you don't want to reveal all your cards too early. Teaching is about pacing. You must know the right time to "reveal" the next step, keeping engagement high while ensuring learning sticks.

For example, imagine you are running an obstacle course with five steps, and you have seven minutes to teach it. If you start with all five steps at once, most students will burn out their engagement after about four minutes. That leaves you with three minutes and a group that has already checked out.

A better way is to take a few minutes on just one step. Provide a lot of praise to those who are doing it correctly, and have the group repeat the step until the energy starts to dip. Then reveal the next step—now they have two. Repeat the process. Add praise. Keep the momentum alive. By the end of seven minutes, you've held their attention, maintained engagement, and made sure the skill transfer stuck.

This method not only fills the time more effectively but also ensures students stay focused and motivated. They feel challenged without being overwhelmed. They also crave the praise that comes with each step of progress.

PRACTICAL APPLICATIONS

Martial Arts Class

You are teaching a group of six-year-olds how to perform a kicking combination. Instead of giving them the full three-step combo right away, start with just the first kick. Once they are engaged and succeeding, add the second kick. Build momentum step by step. If you reveal the whole combo at once, they'll get lost, discouraged, and stop trying.

Classroom

You are teaching long division. Instead of explaining the full multi-step process all at once, take your time with the first step: dividing the first number. Let students work on it, praise them when they succeed, and only then reveal the next part—multiplying, subtracting, and so on. If you show all the steps too soon, the class will feel overwhelmed and lose focus.

Soccer Field

You want your players to learn how to pass and shoot in a drill. Instead of setting up the entire passing-shooting sequence, begin with just the pass. Once they are sharp, add the shot. Finally, add defenders. If you introduce everything at once, they'll fumble and lose engagement.

Parenting at Home

Your child is learning how to clean their room. Instead of dumping the full list—make the bed, put toys away, fold laundry, vacuum—start with one step. Praise them when it's done. Then add the second step. Keep layering until the task is complete. If you reveal the whole list right away, they may shut down and refuse to even start.

Takeaways

- Don't reveal all the steps too early—stretch each phase while students stay engaged.

- Engagement fades fast with younger students, so pacing is critical.

- Use praise at every stage to keep motivation alive.

- Add new steps only when the previous one has been learned.

- The art of teaching is timing: reveal the next "card" at the perfect moment.

MANAGING THE FLOODGATES

When running a drill or game, think of yourself as the operator of a dam. On one side of the dam, there's the powerful energy of your students. On the other side are the floodgates — your ability to control how much freedom they are given at any moment. If you open those gates all the way right from the start, the water will rush uncontrolled and cause damage. But if you use the gates wisely, you can channel that energy into something powerful and productive.

Start Narrow

At the beginning of any drill, your "floodgates" should be almost closed. That means you keep things tight, simple, and highly controlled. You're testing whether students are ready to handle more freedom.

For example, if students are holding paddles for each other, don't just say, "Partner up and start kicking the floor." That's like opening the gates all the way. Instead, begin with control: have them kick once when you call out "Kick." Watch closely — are they holding the paddle properly? Are they kicking responsibly? If not, you know the gates can't open further yet.

Earned Freedom

As students prove themselves, you slowly open the gates wider. You might allow them to kick on their own count, or add multiple kicks before switching partners. The key is that freedom is earned, not given away all at once.

This principle applies across many activities:

- Basketball: Don't start with a full scrimmage. Begin with players dribbling slowly between cones on your command. If they show control, let them dribble faster, then add defenders, then move into a game setting.

- Soccer: Instead of beginning with a free-play match, start with short passing drills in pairs. Once the class shows accuracy and teamwork, expand to small-sided games.

- Classroom learning: In a writing exercise, don't hand students a blank page and say, "Write an essay." Start with a single sentence starter. Once they show understanding, open the gates to a paragraph, then a full essay.

- Music instruction: With beginning guitar players, don't hand them a song to play through all the way. Start with a single chord, transition to two chords, and slowly add rhythm and tempo.

Dialing It Back

Sometimes you'll open the gates too far too quickly — and that's okay. The key is to notice it and dial things back. If students get silly, lose control, or start forgetting technique, narrow the gates again. Bring them back to a simpler version of the drill where you can reset expectations.

The Real Win

The floodgate mindset reminds you that your job isn't just to run drills — it's to manage freedom. By controlling how much independence students have at each stage, you protect the structure of your class and keep students safe, engaged, and learning at the right pace.

Key Takeaway

Start with tight control, give freedom in steps, and be willing to close the gates when needed.

ORGANIZING STUDENTS FOR DRILLS

When it comes to organizing students for drills, speed is everything. Every second spent lining them up or preparing for an activity is a second of lost engagement. Your goal should always be to organize the group as fast as possible so you can get straight into the drill.

The first step is to think before you speak. Ask yourself:

- Where do I want the students to go?

- Do they need partners?

- Do they need gear or equipment like gloves or paddles?

- How should they be spaced?

All of this should be clear in your head before you give any instructions.

When you do give instructions, make them clear and complete. For example, don't just say, "Line up over there." Instead, be specific: "Everyone, line up on the black and gray line next to Mr. Smith." Landmarks save time. You can use assistants, star students, or even yourself as the landmark. For example, "Half of you line up to my right, half to my left—go."

Creativity helps, but clarity is non-negotiable. Use spacing markers like mat increments: "Line up one mat apart" or "Spread out two mats apart." Just make sure students know what that means before using it.

Keep your words short and direct. Filler words only create confusion and waste time. Instead of saying:

"Find a partner who's about your size, grab gloves, line up on this side, one facing this way, the other facing that way."

You can simplify to:

"Find a partner your size. Put on gloves. One on this line, one on that line. Face each other. Go."

Clear and complete instructions paired with urgency keep the flow of class strong. The faster you get students organized, the more time they spend actually learning.

Like anything else, this takes practice. But if you consistently push yourself to be both clear and efficient, you will become a master at organizing students quickly and effectively.

Takeaways

- Speed matters—organize students as quickly as possible to protect engagement.

- Always think through the setup before speaking.

- Use clear, specific, and complete instructions.

- Landmarks (assistants, star students, or yourself) make lining up faster.

- Keep words short and direct—avoid filler.

- Practice clarity and efficiency until it becomes second nature.

THE IMPORTANCE OF FAST REACTION TIME

One of the most crucial expectations I recommend including in every session is for students to react quickly to appropriate requests. Quick reaction time saves valuable minutes, keeps the pace sharp, and ensures the session is productive. More importantly, it trains students to stay alert, listen carefully, and give their best attention.

When a student is in their most focused state, they learn faster and retain information longer. A quick response shows respect, discipline, and confidence. It also communicates mastery because when someone can answer fast, it usually means they really know the material.

Of course, there are moments when you must give a student time to think. But especially with youth in today's fast-paced culture, keeping classes moving quickly works in your favor. If responses are slow, energy drops, engagement fades, and the lesson drags.

At KOMA, our expectation is clear: every student must answer loudly and move fast at all times. Quick reaction time keeps the mind active, the body ready, and the class running with energy. We use every minute of class to its fullest.

In other environments, you may not want students to yell their answers. But I strongly encourage you to have them speak loudly enough to project confidence. Most children naturally speak too softly because they are still developing self-assurance. Training them to respond with volume helps build both confidence and presence.

Quick reaction time applies everywhere—not just in martial arts. In the classroom, it prevents wasted time and creates order. On the soccer field, it keeps practice sharp and players locked in. At home, it establishes respect between parent and child. A request should be acted on now, not later.

The Cost of Slow Reactions

When students respond slowly, you lose momentum.

- The rest of the group is left waiting.

- The energy of the room drops.

- The lesson shifts from active learning to passive waiting.

Slow reactions also weaken respect. If a child learns that they can drag their feet and nothing happens, they will keep doing it. Worse, other students will copy them. Before long, the whole group has lowered its standard.

Quick reactions, on the other hand, raise the bar. They set the tone that expectations matter. They create a culture where focus and discipline are normal, not the exception.

Examples in Action

Martial Arts Class

During a kicking drill, I ask the class to line up. A few students move quickly, but others drag behind. I stop and reset the expectation: "When I say line up, you have five seconds to be in position, standing tall." I repeat the drill, timing them. This time, they move faster. When one student is first, I praise them in front of the group.The others try to beat that time immediately after. The class energy rises, and the drill runs smoothly.

Classroom

A teacher raises her hand as a signal for silence. The first time, it takes 15 seconds for the room to quiet down. She calmly points it out and has them try again. The next time, she praises the first group to respond quickly: "Excellent, this table was ready in just three seconds." The other students now want that recognition, and soon the entire class is responding in three seconds or less.

Parenting at Home

A parent asks their child to put away a toy. The child ignores the request until asked a second or third time. This teaches them that delay is acceptable. Instead, the parent should calmly reset the expectation: "When I ask you to put something away, it should be done right away." The next time, when the child responds quickly, the parent praises them: "Great job listening right away." Over time, the quick reaction becomes the norm.

Building the Habit

You can train fast reaction time just like any other skill:

- Set the expectation clearly. Explain what you want: "When I call your name, answer right away with 'yes.'"

- Time it. Count the seconds out loud if needed. This makes the expectation tangible and measurable.

- Praise the first responder. Public recognition motivates the group to move faster.

- Reset if needed. If reactions are slow, stop and try again until the standard is met.

- Repeat often. The more consistently you reinforce it, the faster it becomes a habit.

Quick reaction time is more than just saving seconds—it's about building respect, order, and discipline. When students learn to react quickly, they not only learn faster in the moment—they also build a habit of focus and discipline that will serve them for life.

Takeaways

- It keeps students alert and fully engaged.

- It prevents wasted time and drifting focus.

- It shows respect when requests are followed immediately.

- It creates momentum, energy, and confidence.

LEADING PRIVATE LESSONS: SIX PRINCIPLES TO FOLLOW

Private lessons are one of the most powerful ways to accelerate a student's growth. They allow for deeper focus, personalized feedback, and faster improvement... but only if the lesson is intentional from start to finish. Every minute counts.

Below are six principles that will help you lead private lessons with clarity, structure, and purpose.

1. Know the Objective Before You Begin

Never start a private lesson without knowing exactly what success looks like. Ask yourself: What should this student be able to do by the end of the lesson?

Sometimes the goal is shared ahead of time by the student or parent— catching up on a form, improving a combination, or preparing for a test or tournament. If no goal is given, use the curriculum as your guide. For example, if the student should already know their form, that becomes your objective.

2. Start Working Toward the Objective Immediately

Begin with purpose. Once the lesson starts, get right into the main focus. Avoid wasting time on small talk, long warmups, or off-topic drills. The student and parent should feel that every moment is directed toward progress.

If the student could use a moment to loosen up, start with a short, upbeat activity to get them ready for the real work.

3. Don't Dwell on Details Too Early

Work on the big pieces first. Once the student can perform the full skill, then go back and refine the smaller parts if time allows. For example, if the goal is to complete an entire form, prioritize flow and memory first. Once they can perform it from start to finish, then they can correct stances, timing, or technique.

4. Eliminate Filler Drills

Every activity in a private lesson must serve the main objective. Stretching, games, or unrelated drills should be used only if they support focus, confidence, or warm-up needs—never as time-fillers.

A good rule: if it doesn't directly help achieve the goal, skip it. Students and parents will notice when time is used wisely.

5. End With a Clear Review

Once the lesson is complete, take one to two minutes to summarize. Review what was *covered* and what was *learned.* For example:

"We went through the entire form today, and you're about 90% of the way there."

This helps the student remember what to work on and assures the parent of the value of the session.

6. Give a Clear Practice Assignment

Always end by setting expectations for what to practice before the next lesson. The next goal should build directly on the one just completed. Example:

"Before we meet again, I need you to be able to perform the entire form without me saying a word."

This turns each private lesson into a step toward long-term mastery rather than random sessions of review.

Takeaways

- Begin every private lesson with a clear, measurable objective.

- Start working toward that goal right away. Don't waste time.

- Focus on mastering the big parts before refining small details.

- Avoid filler drills that don't support the lesson goal.

- End each lesson with a review of what was covered and learned.

- Give a specific practice task that connects to the next objective.

- Stay focused, structured, and intentional. The student should leave every lesson feeling progress and clarity.

PART 8D

RELATIONSHIP TOOLS

HELPING NEW STUDENTS FEEL WELCOME

The first few classes a new student attends can make or break their entire experience and perception of your program. If those early moments go well, the student is more likely to stay engaged and committed. If they don't, the student may quickly lose interest and never return. That's why one of the most important responsibilities of an instructor is to make new students feel welcome.

The process starts the moment they walk into the studio. Observe their behavior right away. Are they shy? Are they hyper? Are they nervous? These first impressions give you the clues you need on how to approach them.

Your initial approach should always be humble and calm. Never come across as too aggressive or overly energetic. Even if some students might enjoy that personality, others—especially shy or introverted youth—will feel overwhelmed or intimidated. Instead, keep your voice softer, your body language open, and maintain space so they don't feel crowded. Small things like keeping your hands behind your back, bending slightly forward, and speaking gently can go a long way in helping a new student feel safe.

Start with light, simple questions: "What's your favorite color?" "What's your favorite food?" "What did you do today?" Keep it fun and easy. But don't overdo it. If the student looks uncomfortable, don't keep pressing. Sometimes it's best to simply smile and let a little silence settle so they can adjust to the new environment.

One of the most effective ways to help a student feel connected is to introduce them to other students who are about the same age and gender. That connection with peers can be the difference between a student feeling like an outsider or feeling like they belong. Just be careful not to embarrass them by drawing too much attention. Avoid introductions to the entire class at once, which can feel overwhelming. Instead, create small, natural introductions to one or two students who can help ease them in.

As class progresses, keep an eye on the new student. Do they look comfortable? Are they engaging with others? Do they look tense or awkward? If so, step in again—make another introduction or start another small conversation. Sometimes one positive connection is all it takes for a new student to feel relaxed and ready to participate.

Your responsibility as an instructor is to take care of that student from the moment they start. Make sure they feel connected. Make sure they feel relaxed. And most importantly, make sure they feel taken care of. A strong first impression will create a foundation of trust and engagement that lasts far beyond their first few classes.

Takeaways

- First impressions set the tone for the entire student experience.

- Approach new students with humility and calm, not over-the-top energy.

- Use light, simple questions to build a connection—but avoid overwhelming them.

- Introduce them to peers of similar age and gender to create a sense of belonging.

- Keep watch throughout the class and step in as needed to ensure they feel connected and cared for.

KEEPING THE CONNECTION STRONG WITH LARGE GROUPS

It's easy to connect with every student when you only have a handful in class. But when the group grows larger, the challenge increases. Without intentional effort, students can easily slip through the cracks, and once a student feels invisible, their engagement and motivation quickly fade. The solution is not to work harder but to work smarter, using proven habits that help you maintain personal connections even in a crowded room.

1. Prioritize Eye Contact

The most straightforward and most powerful tool you have is eye contact. It communicates, "I see you. I notice you. You matter." In a small group, this happens naturally. In a large group, discipline is required. Make it a goal to give every student a moment of eye contact during the class. Even two seconds of connection can be enough to keep a student engaged.

Think of it as scanning but locking in, not just looking past. Instead of sweeping your eyes across the room, pause on individual students. This helps them feel recognized and keeps their attention locked on you.

2. Use Physical Presence

Your voice is important, but your presence is what carries authority and connection. Picture your students as cell phone towers and yourself as the phone. The closer you get, the stronger the signal. If you stay at the front of the class the entire time, you lose the chance to connect deeply with those in the back or corners. Move around deliberately—stand near different groups, pause next to quieter students, and make your presence felt throughout the room.

Your physical presence also communicates accountability. When you're nearby, students tend to focus more. Walking the floor reminds them you're watching, and it reassures them that you care.

3. Create Individual Touch Points

Large groups make it easy for some students to disappear. That's why it's crucial to intentionally speak to each student at least once during class. This doesn't mean long conversations—it can be as simple as a correction, a quick question, or encouragement. Phrases like "Nice work," "Can you rotate your wrist?" or "Good focus today" go a long way.

For students who tend to fade into the background, a small acknowledgment can completely change how they feel about class. When a child hears their name spoken positively in a room of twenty or thirty, it reminds them they are seen and valued.

4. Break the Group into Smaller Units

Another way to manage connections is by structuring the class so that the group feels smaller. This can be done through partner drills, small group challenges, or even assigning assistants to help monitor and encourage sections of the class. While you cannot give every student equal attention at the same time, you can design the class so that everyone experiences attention from either you or an assistant.

5. Balance Energy Across the Room

In large groups, it's natural to gravitate toward the louder or more engaged students, but this leaves others overlooked. Make a conscious effort to spread your energy evenly. If you've given praise on one side of the room, walk to the opposite side to do the same. If you've asked a question to an outspoken student, follow up with a quieter one. This balance ensures no one feels left out.

6. Stay Consistent

Connection in large groups isn't a one-time effort. It has to be maintained throughout the entire class. That means constant scanning, moving, and interacting. It's exhausting at first, but once you develop the rhythm, it becomes second nature.

Takeaway

A large group doesn't have to weaken your connection with students. Through intentional habits—eye contact, physical presence, personal touch points, breaking groups into smaller units, and balancing energy—you can ensure that every student feels seen, valued, and engaged, no matter how big the class grows.

ELEVATING YOUR ASSISTANT

One of the best feelings an instructor can have is leading a class with a capable assistant by their side. A good assistant can make the class flow smoothly, reduce stress on the lead instructor, and ensure that every student receives more attention. But an assistant can also make or break the experience. If they are left standing in the corner doing nothing, they quickly lose motivation and, before long, may not even want to help anymore.

It is your responsibility as the lead instructor to keep assistants engaged. Think of them the same way you think of students—because in many ways, they are. You would never let a student stand around disengaged and bored. The same applies to your assistant. The end goal is for every assistant to become confident enough to lead a class on their own. That means you must give them live training during your class, using your best judgment on when and how.

Sometimes this means letting them count aloud and practice their voice. Other times, it might be letting them lead a warm-up game, hold paddles, or manage a small group for a short drill. These opportunities must be intentional, but they also must be balanced with what the parents in the lobby are seeing.

At KOMA, we distinguish between two types of assistants: the **assistant instructor** and the **Mentorship assistant** (our name for youth assistants in training).

- Mentorship Assistants (young assistants) should mainly serve as role models and helpers. They can demonstrate techniques in front of the class, gather paddles or equipment, hold pads, or lead very small groups for only a few minutes at a time. The goal is to give them exposure and responsibility without ever making it look like a child is teaching half the class.

- Assistant Instructors (more advanced assistants) can take on more. They can lead small groups of three to five students for up to 10 minutes if they've earned your trust. They can also run warm-ups, count for drills, and even manage short sections of class. But this still requires careful judgment—new assistants should be given shorter, simpler tasks until they show consistency.

Everything comes down to two questions:

1. Is this task appropriate for their level of training?

2. What does this look like to the parents who are watching?

If parents see an assistant who is confident, engaging, and clearly under your guidance, it strengthens their trust in your program. But if they see a young mentorship student running half the class alone, that trust can disappear quickly.

Never forget: it is your responsibility to train assistants just as much as it is your responsibility to train students. Keep them engaged, give them opportunities to grow, and elevate them step by step until they can lead like you. When you do this, you aren't just running a smoother class—you're building the next generation of instructors.

Takeaways

- Assistants should never stand idle—keep them engaged.

- KOMA calls young assistants Mentorship assistants—use them as role models, not teachers.

- Assistant instructors can lead small groups but only after earning trust.

- Always consider how parents will perceive the assistant's role.

- Your job is to train assistants to replace you one day.

SPEAKING TO PARENTS

Speaking with parents is one of the most critical responsibilities of an instructor. Parents are trusting you with the most valuable thing in their lives—their child. The way you handle these conversations can either build confidence in you or create doubt.

The Basics

When speaking with parents, keep these do's and don'ts in mind:

- Stay Positive – Never tell a parent they need to "fix" their child's behavior. That is why they brought their child to you. Your role is to focus on character development and guide them toward the right behaviors.

- Speak Clearly and Confidently – Use a humble tone. Confidence without arrogance builds trust.

- Listen More Than You Speak – Parents will often tell you what they value most if you give them space.

- Keep It Concise – Say enough to be clear, but avoid rambling.

- Don't Guess – If you're unsure about an answer, say: "Let me check on that and get back to you." This shows honesty, not weakness.

Addressing Shortcomings

Curriculum Struggles

If a student is falling behind, avoid framing it as the parent's responsibility to "fix." Saying "You need to practice an hour every day at home" communicates that we failed in class.

Instead, try this:

- "You've probably noticed your son is struggling a little with the material. We're going to do everything we can in class to help him progress. If you'd like to make the experience even smoother, he could practice just 10 minutes at home for the next few days."

This frames practice as an enhancement rather than a burden, and it keeps the instructor accountable.

Attendance Inconsistency

When addressing missed classes, tread carefully. Parents already feel guilty about inconsistency.

- Start positive: "Brian, great to see you today!"

- Raise the concern gently: "I noticed I haven't seen you consistently these last couple of weeks. Is everything okay?"

- Give options: "Do our current class times still work, or would another slot be easier for your schedule?"

- End encouragingly: "Remember, consistent attendance is what will help you feel most prepared to earn your next belt."

Stop there. Don't push further. The goal is to remind, not to shame.

Building Rapport

Rapport builds trust, and trust is the foundation of working with parents.

- Ask simple questions about the parent or child.

- Listen more than you speak.

- Be knowledgeable about your program so they see you as a resource.

Advanced Shortcomings with Scripts

1. Behavior Issues

How to address it without labeling the child:

- Wrong: "Your son is disrespectful in class."

- Right: "I've noticed a few moments where he struggled to focus and follow instructions in class. Here's how we're working on it: when he gets distracted, we bring him back with eye contact and a simple cue. If you'd like, you could use the same cue at home — something like 'focus time' — so he hears a consistent message."

This keeps the responsibility with the instructor while inviting the parent into a supportive role.

2. Motivation Drop

Script for a student who says they don't want to come anymore: "It's normal for kids to feel a dip in motivation. The exciting part is helping them push through, because that's where real growth happens. For now, let's set a short-term goal. How about we help him earn his next stripe? That way, he'll feel a win without thinking too far ahead."

Alternate script if parent is panicking: "Please don't worry — almost every student hits this phase. What usually helps is mixing things up. We'll involve him in more partner drills and make sure he feels connected. Often, just one or two good classes reignites motivation."

3. Parent Frustrations

When a parent complains about progress:

- Parent: "I don't think my daughter is learning fast enough."

- Instructor: "I completely understand how you feel. We both want her to succeed and stay motivated. What I can tell you is that progress in martial arts often comes in waves. Sometimes it looks like little growth, then suddenly there's a breakthrough. Right now, we're focusing on building her foundation so that the next breakthrough will be strong."

This method of agree, align, and redirect validates the parent while still keeping authority.

4. Sensitive Family Struggles

When outside factors are affecting class performance: "I can only imagine how tough things must be at home right now. Please know we'll do everything we can to keep this a safe and consistent place for him. Our goal is that when he walks through the doors, he feels supported and confident."

Keep it private. Show empathy. Always redirect back to the program as a place of stability and care.

Takeaway

Speaking with parents creates space to show you're invested in their child's learning and well-being. Keep conversations positive, specific, and solution-focused. When shortcomings appear, address them with grace, tact, and scripts that build trust rather than create tension.

PART 9

ADDRESSING BEHAVIOR

ADDRESSING BEHAVIOR

Every instructor, no matter how skilled, will face moments when students test the limits. A child talks while you're giving directions. A teenager rolls their eyes at a correction. An adult looks distracted and tunes out. These situations can challenge you, providing openings to demonstrate leadership.

Addressing behavior is one of the defining marks of a great instructor. Anyone can run drills when everyone is cooperating. But true leadership shows up when things aren't going smoothly. The way you respond in these moments sets the tone for the entire class.

Handled poorly, corrections create tension, embarrassment, or even resentment. Handled well, corrections create structure, trust, and respect. The key is understanding that addressing behavior is not about "winning" against the student. It's about guiding them back into alignment with the standards of the group so everyone can learn and grow.

Many new instructors avoid addressing behavior altogether, hoping the problem goes away. Or, they swing too hard in the opposite direction, coming down with unnecessary force. Both extremes weaken your leadership. The goal is to find the balance: calm, clear, and consistent.

In this chapter, we'll cover why addressing behavior matters, how to do it without drama, and the specific approaches you can use to correct in a way that builds respect instead of fear. By the end, you'll come to see that what feels like a disruption is actually a key part of the learning process.

THE PURPOSE OF ADDRESSING BEHAVIOR

One of the most important skills you will ever develop as an instructor is the ability to address behavior. Every student will eventually test the boundaries of what is acceptable. How you respond in those moments determines not only whether order is restored but also whether respect is earned.

The purpose of addressing behavior is not to embarrass, punish, or dominate the student. The purpose is to guide them back on track so learning can continue. When done well, addressing behavior strengthens respect, improves engagement, and keeps the learning environment healthy for everyone.

Many instructors struggle with this. Some avoid it completely because they want to be liked, falling into the Tippy Toe Method. Others overdo it, relying on fear and intimidation like the Authoritative Method. Both approaches miss the mark. The real goal is not to avoid or to dominate—it's to confront with clarity and respect.

Why It Matters

Every group needs structure. Without clear standards, students become distracted, push limits, and lose focus. If one student misbehaves and the instructor does nothing, the rest of the group notices. Soon, behavior spreads. In contrast, when an instructor quickly and respectfully addresses behavior, the entire group learns two things:

- Expectations matter.

- The instructor is paying attention.

The faster the behavior is addressed, the stronger the message. Small problems left unchecked turn into bigger problems. Correcting in the moment prevents issues from multiplying.

Respect Through Accountability

Students respect instructors who hold them accountable. It shows you care enough not to let them drift. In fact, students often push limits just to see if the instructor will notice. When you step in with calm authority, it reassures them. It tells them, "I see you, I care about you, and I expect better from you."

Respect built this way lasts much longer than respect built on fear. Students know you are consistent. They know you mean what you say. And they know you are guiding them for their good—not just to satisfy your own ego.

The Bigger Picture

Addressing behavior is not about stopping misbehavior—it's about shaping character. When you teach a child to respond quickly, listen respectfully, or follow through with effort, you are teaching life lessons that go beyond the classroom or training hall. These lessons shape how they interact with teachers, bosses, teammates, and even their own families one day.

This is why addressing behavior is so important. It is not a side task—it is the core of teaching. Skills and drills matter, but if the student never learns respect, focus, or self-control, those skills will not last.

Takeaways

- Addressing behavior keeps order and protects the learning environment.

- The goal is not punishment but guidance back on track.

- Quick correction prevents small problems from growing.

- Accountability earns real respect.

- Addressing behavior today helps shape the student's character for tomorrow.

CONFRONTATION WITHOUT DRAMA

When most people hear the word confrontation, they think of conflict, tension, or raised voices. But confrontation does not have to mean drama. In fact, the most effective confrontation is calm, clear, and professional. The purpose is not to embarrass or punish the student—it is to reset the standard and keep learning on track.

The key is remembering this truth: behavior that goes unaddressed will repeat itself. If you ignore it once, the student believes it's acceptable. If you ignore it twice, it becomes the new standard. Every time you let behavior slide, you lower the bar for the whole group. Confrontation is your responsibility to protect the standard.

The mistake many instructors make is waiting until they are frustrated before they act. By then, their body language, tone, and words come out sharp. That's when confrontation turns into drama. The best instructors address behavior early, before emotions rise.

Here's the formula:

1. Notice quickly. The faster you catch it, the lighter the confrontation can be.

2. Stay calm. Keep your tone steady, posture relaxed, and facial expression neutral.

3. Be clear. State or ask exactly what expectation was missed, without extra emotion.

4. Reset. Have the student do it again correctly so they leave with success, not failure.

Case Studies in Action

- Martial arts class: A student responds slowly to "line up." Instead of snapping, the instructor calmly says, "That was too slow. Can you move faster?" The group repeats, and the new standard is reinforced.

- Classroom: A student blurts out without raising their hand. The teacher pauses, makes eye contact, and asks, "What's our rule when someone else is speaking?" The student corrects themselves, and the lesson continues without losing rhythm.

- Soccer field: A player dribbles as the coach gives instructions. Instead of shouting, the coach walks over, places a hand on the ball, and says quietly, "Can you focus your eyes on me when I'm talking?" The player stops, nods, and focuses.

- Home: A child ignores the parent's request to put shoes away. Instead of yelling, the parent calmly asks, "What are we supposed to do with our shoes?" The child sighs but picks them up. The standard is upheld without conflict.

In each case, the instructor or parent confronts directly but without added emotion. The focus stays on the behavior, not the person.

Why It Works

Students actually feel safer when you confront them consistently. It shows them you are steady, in control, and reliable. Drama communicates the opposite—it makes students unsure of what you'll do next. Calm confrontation proves you value the standard more than your own comfort, which builds lasting respect.

Common Mistakes to Avoid

- Sarcasm. Sarcasm may feel like a lighter way to correct, but it often confuses or embarrasses the student. Clarity always works better.

- Lecturing. A long lecture turns a small issue into a big scene. Say less, act more. Reset the behavior quickly.

- Public shaming. Correcting loudly with the goal of humiliating the student damages trust. Direct but respectful correction builds respect.

- Waiting too long. Delaying confrontation lets frustration build up in you, and bad habits build up in the student. The longer you wait, the harder it becomes to correct.

- Overreacting. Small problems don't need big reactions. If you explode, the drama overshadows the lesson.

Takeaways

- Confrontation is not about conflict—it's about protecting the standard.

- Address behavior early, before frustration grows.

- Stay calm, clear, and neutral.

- Reset the behavior with action, not lecture.

- Avoid sarcasm, lecturing, public shaming, waiting too long, and overreacting.

- Students respect leaders who confront without drama.

PREPARING TO ADDRESS BEHAVIOR

Addressing inappropriate behavior can feel like one of the most difficult challenges instructors face. At times, it may seem almost impossible to overcome without losing patience or control. The good news is this: addressing behavior is a skill like any other. With the right strategies and enough practice, you can become confident and effective at handling even the toughest situations.

One strategy you should **never** use is ignoring inappropriate behavior until it stops. Hoping it goes away on its own rarely works. In fact, ignoring it often teaches the opposite lesson—students begin to believe their behavior has no consequence. All inappropriate behavior should be addressed swiftly, directly, and with composure.

Most people naturally avoid confrontation because it feels awkward or uncomfortable. But the faster you overcome this hesitation, the stronger you will become as a leader. Avoiding confrontation weakens authority; addressing it builds trust and order.

Before you can effectively address behavior, two important objectives must be established early in class.

1. Establish Authority

Within the first ten minutes, students must recognize you as the leader of the class. If they don't, every attempt at correction will feel like a negotiation. Authority doesn't mean yelling or intimidating. It means calmly but firmly making it clear that you are in charge and the structure of the session will be respected.

2. Establish Connection

Along with authority, you must build a personal connection with each student. When students feel connected to you, they also feel a sense of obligation to comply. Think about it: people are far more likely to help or cooperate with someone they know personally than with a stranger. Even small moments of eye contact, a smile, or asking a student about their day create the connection you need.

When both authority and connection are in place, students are much more likely to listen, comply, and respond when you address behavior.

From here, the next step is developing **emotional control**. No matter what a student does, you must remain calm, positive, and confident. Losing emotional control—raising your voice out of anger, showing frustration, or appearing rattled—undermines your authority instantly. The students will interpret it as a sign that you can't handle leading them. Staying calm, even when you're firm, communicates strength and steadiness.

It's also important to remember what's really happening when a student chooses inappropriate behavior. At the core, the student simply wants something different than what you're asking for. That's it. Behavior challenges are less about disrespect and more about conflicting goals. This perspective helps you approach the situation with clarity rather than frustration.

The best instructors adopt a **win-win mindset**. This doesn't mean giving in to the student's every demand. It means asking yourself: What can I give the student that still upholds the rules and integrity of the class? Sometimes it's as small as acknowledgment, redirection, or an opportunity to try again. Seeing the moment through the eyes of the student helps you respond with both firmness and empathy.

In review, here are the key steps in preparing to address behavior:

- Overcome the fear of confrontation.

- Establish authority within the first ten minutes.

- Establish a connection with every student early in class.

- Develop strong emotional control—never lose composure.

- Adopt a win-win mindset, always seeking solutions that uphold structure while meeting students where they are.

When you prepare in these ways, every strategy you use to address behavior will work better. You'll respond with clarity, confidence, and consistency, and your students will respect both your authority and your care.

THE TWO TYPES OF APPROACHES

When it comes to addressing behavior, there are two main approaches every instructor should understand: the **Reminder Approach** and the **Conversation Approach**. You'll notice these aren't completely new concepts—you've already seen hints of them in earlier sections when we discussed quick corrections versus deeper conversations. Now we're going to formalize these into specific tools you can deploy systematically.

The Reminder Approach

Most first-time occurrences of inappropriate behavior should be handled with the Reminder Approach. This is for minor behaviors that are not dangerous to the student or others. Examples include talking during class, not standing in line correctly, or goofing off with another student.

Just like the name suggests, this approach is nothing more than a quick, clear reminder. You calmly remind the student that their behavior is not acceptable and that it needs to change right away. The goal here is speed—correct it and move on. You can also provide a confused look as a reminder to the student. We will cover that approach in more depth later.

The Reminder Approach works best when it's short and sharp. But it should not be overused with the same student. If you keep giving reminders without changing your approach, the student will eventually tune you out. At that point, the reminder loses its power.

The Conversation Approach

When the behavior is more substantial, or when reminders no longer work, you need the Conversation Approach. This is for bigger issues such as hitting another student, running dangerously close to a wall, or showing outright defiance.

What makes the Conversation Approach different is that it begins with a question. Instead of simply telling the student what to do, you ask something that forces them to think. Their brain must engage at a deeper level before they choose what to do next.

This matters because when students choose for themselves, the lesson sticks. Autonomy, or having ownership over their choice, is a powerful motivator. All people, regardless of age, are more committed to the decisions they make themselves than the ones handed to them.

Keep It Short

Regardless of which approach you use, the interaction should be as short as possible. Every second you spend addressing one student is a second you're not leading the rest of the group. Long corrections pull attention away from those who are behaving well and give too much spotlight to the student who is not.

A good rule of thumb is this: keep all reminders and conversations to 20 seconds or less. The faster you correct, the faster you can return your focus to the group. Your priority should always be to give most of your attention to the students who are showing the right behavior, not to the one student who is not.

Now that you know the difference between reminders and conversations, the next step is learning how to use each one effectively.

Takeaways

- Use the Reminder Approach for minor, first-time issues.

- Use the Conversation Approach for serious behavior or when reminders fail.

- The Reminder Approach is fast and corrective.

- The Conversation Approach engages the student's brain by asking questions.

- Keep both approaches under 20 seconds to maintain class flow.

- Always give more attention to students who are doing the right thing.

THE CONFUSED LOOK APPROACH

The Confused Look Approach is a Reminder Approach that uses your expression—not your words—to guide a student back on track.

When a student is not doing what they're supposed to, pause and give them a calm, puzzled look. This silent reminder communicates that something doesn't make sense. Most of the time, you don't have to say anything—the look itself speaks for you. Students will usually pause, think, and correct themselves.

Your facial expression is what makes it work. Tilt your head slightly, purse your lips, and furrow your eyebrows just enough to show genuine confusion— not anger or frustration. The goal is curiosity, not confrontation.

Make sure your face actually looks confused. Many instructors *think* they do, but they don't. Check in the mirror or ask trusted teammates for feedback to confirm that your look reads clearly.

This approach only works if the student feels two things: **connection** and **authority**. The student must feel that you care about them and know who they are, but also that you are firmly in charge. Without that balance, your look may come across as frustration or sarcasm instead of guidance.

You can add a short, calm question if needed, such as:

- "Is that how we stand right now?"

- "Hmm, what's going on here?"

But often, you don't need to say a word. The look alone communicates correction.

Takeaways

- The Confused Look Approach is a Reminder Approach that corrects through expression, not words.

- Tilt your head, purse your lips, and furrow your eyebrows to show genuine confusion.

- Check in the mirror or ask for feedback to ensure your look reads correctly.

- Only works if the student feels both connection and authority from you.

- Keep it calm, curious, and silent—your face often says enough.

- Quick, subtle, and powerful—it helps students self-correct without conflict.

THE CAVE MAN METHOD

The Cave Man Method is a Reminder Approach that uses sound and body language instead of words. It's simple, quick, and often surprisingly effective.

When you notice a student behaving inappropriately, you don't need to lecture or explain. Instead, make direct eye contact and give a short, guttural sound—something you'd imagine a caveman making before language existed. For example: "Ah! Ah! Ah!"

It may feel silly at first, but that's part of what makes it work. The sound is unexpected. It grabs the student's attention and makes them pause to think, "Why is my instructor doing that?" That moment of curiosity gives them the space to adjust their behavior without you having to say more.

Keep your expression and body language positive. Lift your eyebrows slightly, keep your tone light, and avoid any sign of anger or sarcasm. You want it to communicate, "I see what you're doing, and that's not okay," without shaming or embarrassing the student.

You can add a small hand gesture to make it even more straightforward. For example, lift your palm up and gently motion toward the correct behavior while repeating the sound. If a student is out of line or slouching, a few short "Ah! Ah!" sounds with a hand signal are often all it takes to reset them.

This approach works because it's quick, simple, and nonverbal. It keeps the class moving, prevents over-talking, and avoids giving too much attention to negative behavior.

Takeaways

- The Cave Man Method is a **Reminder Approach** that uses sound and presence instead of words.

- Make eye contact and give a short, repeating sound like "Ah! Ah! Ah!"

- Keep your tone light and your facial expression positive.

- Add a calm, palm-up gesture to guide the correct behavior.

- Avoid lecturing—the power is in the pause and the surprise.

- Quick, simple, and nonverbal—it resets behavior without slowing the class.

The Repeating Nope Approach is a Reminder Approach that is one of the simplest reminder strategies you can use when addressing inappropriate behavior.

As soon as you notice a student not behaving appropriately, you simply repeat the word "Nope" over and over again in a steady rhythm:

"Nope. Nope. Nope. Nope. Nope. Nope."

Why does this work? First, it cuts through distractions. Often, when we say something once, it doesn't register. The student may be distracted, caught up in the noise around them, or simply not paying attention. But when you repeat the word several times, it forces their brain to shift gears and recognize the cue. By the fourth, fifth, or sixth "Nope," they almost always hear it.

Second, the repetition creates a small sense of annoyance—not in a harsh way, but just enough to interrupt the behavior. The student begins to wonder, "Why is my instructor saying this over and over again?" That pause is often all that's needed to redirect them.

The key to making this work is how you deliver it. Keep your body language relaxed and your expression positive. Lift your eyebrows slightly and stay calm. If you come across as frustrated or mocking, the method loses its power and may even create resistance.

For example:

- If a student is sitting incorrectly, you can point with your palm up while saying, "Nope. Nope. Nope."

- If two students are goofing off together, make eye contact and calmly repeat, "Nope. Nope. Nope." until they stop.

Be consistent in how it sounds. Your goal is a steady, almost neutral tone with a hint of positivity:

"Nope. Nope. Nope. Nope. Nope."

Avoid exaggerating it into a sarcastic or condescending tone, such as:

"No, no, no, no, nooo..."

That comes across as mocking and will likely backfire.

Remember, this is a reminder approach, not a conversation approach. You are not trying to engage the student in dialogue. Instead, you are giving a quick, light correction that doesn't slow the class down.

Takeaways

- Repeat "Nope" in a steady, consistent rhythm.

- Stay positive in tone, facial expression, and body language.

- Use it as a quick reminder, not a lecture.

- Don't overdo it—avoid sounding sarcastic or obnoxious.

- Keep moving forward with the lesson once the behavior stops.

THE OPEN-ENDED QUESTION APPROACH

One of the most powerful Conversational Approaches for addressing inappropriate behavior is the Open-Ended Question Approach.

Instead of telling the student what they did wrong, you ask them a question that forces them to think for themselves. An open-ended question cannot be answered with a simple "yes" or "no." It allows the student to respond in their own words and, more importantly, to reflect on their behavior.

For example, you might ask:

- "What should you be doing right now?"

- "How do you think that choice is affecting the rest of the group?"

- "What's the right way to handle this situation?"

These questions are effective because they require the student to pause, process, and choose a response. If a student is slouching when they should be sitting tall, asking, "What should you be doing right now?" nudges them to self-correct without you having to lecture. Ideally, the student doesn't just answer with words—they show you through their actions.

This approach works because ownership matters. People, no matter their age, are more engaged with ideas they feel they own. When the answer comes from their own mouth—or is expressed through their own action—they are more likely to follow through and remember it.

That said, open-ended questions can take more time. Students may hesitate, stall, or get stuck. You don't want to wait too long, especially in a group setting, because the rest of the class loses momentum. If the student struggles, you can guide them by narrowing the choices. This shifts into the Closed-Ended Question Approach, which we'll cover in the next chapter.

Keep your questions short and precise. Overloading students with multiple questions at once only confuses them and drags out the correction.

Instead of saying:

"What should you be doing now and why are you doing it?"

You simply say:

"What should you be doing right now?"

Your word choice matters. The quality of your question often determines the quality of the response. Think carefully about how you phrase your question so it directs the student's attention toward the behavior you want to see.

When used well, the Open-Ended Question Approach shifts the responsibility back to the student. Instead of you telling them what to do, they discover it themselves—and that is far more powerful for lasting growth.

Takeaways

- Use open-ended questions to encourage students to think for themselves.

- Keep questions short, clear, and direct.

- Don't wait too long for answers—guide if needed.

- Aim for the student to show the right behavior, not just say it.

- Remember: ownership leads to lasting change.

THE CLOSED-ENDED QUESTION APPROACH

Another effective Conversational Approach for addressing inappropriate behavior is the Closed-Ended Question Approach.

Unlike open-ended questions, which allow students to respond in many different ways, closed-ended questions give them a limited set of choices. This makes it faster, simpler, and easier for the student to clearly see the difference between the right and wrong behaviors.

For example:

- "Should you be sitting or standing right now?"

- "Should you be standing like this, or like this?"

The student only has two options, which makes the expectation clear. This approach works because:

1. The student must think about their behavior and choose between the options.

2. It saves time because you can guide them toward the correct behavior quickly.

To be effective, don't provide too many choices. If you ask:

"Should you be sitting, standing, on one knee, on two knees, or in a kicking stance?"

The student will get confused or forget half the options. Keep it to two, maybe three at most.

Also, make the options polar opposites so the right answer is obvious. For example: "Should you be sitting on two knees or lying on your side right now?"

This forces the student to see the clear contrast between correct and incorrect behavior.

Closed-ended questions are especially useful when:

- You need a quick correction.

- The student struggles to answer open-ended questions.

- You want to speed up the decision-making process without slowing down the whole group.

By mastering the Closed-Ended Question Approach, you gain another quick and effective tool for addressing inappropriate behavior while keeping the class moving forward.

Takeaways

- Closed-ended questions give students clear, limited choices.

- Keep the options short—two is ideal.

- Use polar opposites so the correct behavior stands out.

- This approach is fast, simple, and helps students choose the right action without confusion.

THE CONFUSED QUESTION APPROACH

The Confused Question Approach is a Conversational Approach that helps correct behavior calmly and effectively. Instead of telling a student they're wrong, you guide them to realize it themselves through curiosity and reflection.

This approach is best used after you've already had a conversation about the behavior and the student understands the expectations. The Confused Look is a first reminder. The Confused Question comes later, when expectations have already been discussed and agreed upon, but the behavior still slips.

Here's how it works. When you notice a student making the wrong choice, don't lecture or raise your voice. Simply look a little puzzled and ask a short, direct question that begins with, "I'm a little confused..."

Examples:

- "I'm a little confused. I thought we already agreed this isn't how we behave in class."

- "I'm a little confused. I thought you knew we were supposed to stay in line. Am I correct or not?"

Your tone should be calm, and your facial expression should be genuinely curious, not angry, sarcastic, or overly cheerful. This mix of calm tone and puzzled look makes the student stop and think: "Why is my instructor confused about what I'm doing?" That moment of reflection often leads them to fix their behavior on their own.

After you ask the question, stop talking. Let the silence do the work. The pause gives the student time to think, reflect, and respond. Most of the time, they'll admit they know the proper behavior and correct it.

You can strengthen this approach by connecting it to something you've already said:

"I'm a little confused. Didn't we just talk about staying focused during drills?"

This reinforces prior expectations and helps the student take ownership.

Takeaways

- The Confused Question Approach is a Conversational Approach used after expectations have been clearly discussed and agreed upon.

- The Confused Look is the first reminder; the Confused Question is the next step if behavior continues.

- Keep your tone calm and your expression curious, not frustrated.

- Ask short, clear questions that begin with "I'm a little confused..."

- Pause and let the silence create space for reflection.

- Connect the question to previous expectations to encourage accountability.

- Simple, calm, and direct approaches promote self-correction without conflict.

THE APOLOGY AND THANK YOU APPROACH

The Apology and Thank You Approach is a Conversational Approach that works because it is both polite and disarming. It keeps the instructor calm, positive, and in control while prompting the student to correct their behavior respectfully.

Here's how it works. As soon as you notice a student displaying inappropriate behavior, you approach them for a quick one-on-one exchange. Your words might sound like this:

"I'm sorry, I thought we had already agreed that touching other students in line wasn't appropriate. Is that something you can stop doing for the rest of class?"

The student then responds, usually with a "yes." You immediately close with:

"Thank you, sir." or "Thank you, ma'am."

And then you walk away.

This short exchange is powerful for a few reasons:

- Starting with an apology gets the student's attention. When someone apologizes to us, our brain instantly wants to know why. It lowers defenses and makes the student more willing to listen.

- Stating the behavior clearly leaves no confusion about what needs to change.

- Asking for agreement ("Is that something you can stop doing?") gives the student a choice, which strengthens their accountability.

- Closing with thank you ends the conversation politely and respectfully, reinforcing that you are calm and in control.

The key is to avoid sounding condescending. For example, saying, "I'm sorry, I thought I already told you not to touch people in class. What's going on here? Could you please stop?" can sound frustrated or sarcastic. This tone undermines the effectiveness of your message.

Instead, keep your tone polite, respectful, and steady. Facial expression matters here, too. Keep your body language relaxed, your eyebrows up, and your tone even.

Because this approach requires precision, practice it ahead of time. Stand in front of a mirror, record yourself, or role-play with a colleague. The more confident and natural you are, the more effective it will be.

Takeaways

- The Apology and Thank You Approach is a Conversational Approach that corrects behavior in a calm, respectful manner.

- Begin with a sincere apology to lower the student's defenses and gain attention.

- State the behavior clearly so there is no confusion about what needs to change.

- Ask for agreement to give the student ownership and accountability.

- End with a polite "Thank you, sir/ma'am" to close the exchange with respect.

- Keep your tone steady, polite, and never sarcastic.

- Practice in advance so your delivery feels natural and confident.

- When done correctly, this approach corrects behavior without conflict and strengthens the relationship between instructor and student.

THE I NEED YOUR HELP APPROACH

One of the most powerful ways to address inappropriate behavior is the "I Need Your Help" Approach. This Conversational Approach reframes correction as a request for leadership, thereby building respect rather than resistance.

Here's how it works. As soon as you notice a student not giving their best effort or engaging in inappropriate behavior, approach them calmly for a brief conversation. It might sound like this:

"Sir, I need your help with something. You're one of the highest belts in the class, and I look at you as a leader. But when you step up to kick the paddle, it doesn't seem like you're giving your best effort. Could you help me by showing the class your best effort every time? That way, the rest of the class will also start trying harder. Could you do that favor for me?"

Now, the student has to answer yes or no. Most students will say yes. When they do, finish with an energetic, respectful close:

"Thank you, sir. I really appreciate that. Go ahead and return to your line."

This approach works because:

- It elevates responsibility. By asking for help, you frame the student as someone important, not just someone who needs correction.

- It builds leadership. Students often rise to the challenge when they believe others are looking up to them.

- It stays respectful. Instead of scolding, you invite the student into partnership.

But there's a warning: this approach only works if you are authentic. If you sound fake, condescending, or uninterested, it will backfire.

Compare these two tones:

- Authentic: "I need your help. Could you give your best effort so the class can follow your example?"

- Fake: "I need your help... you're not giving your best effort, so can you just try harder?"

The first feels genuine. The second feels dismissive. The difference is in tone, body language, and authenticity.

That's why practice is key. Rehearse in front of a mirror, record yourself on video, or role-play with another instructor until your delivery is sharp, confident, and natural. The more authentic you are, the more effective this approach becomes.

Takeaways

- The I Need Your Help Approach is a Conversational Approach that turns correction into leadership.

- Begin with a calm, respectful tone and genuine eye contact.

- Ask for help instead of giving orders—it raises the student's sense of responsibility.

- Frame the student as a leader whose actions influence others.

- Keep your message positive and focused on teamwork, not blame.

- End with gratitude: "Thank you, sir/ma'am. I really appreciate that."

- This approach only works if your tone is authentic and sincere—never sarcastic or forced.

- Practice your delivery so it feels natural, confident, and genuine.

- When done right, this approach builds respect, strengthens connections, and inspires better behavior through leadership.

THE THREE ADDRESS RULE

What do you do if you are constantly having to address inappropriate behavior with the same student? The Three Address Rule gives you a straightforward process to follow so you stay consistent, fair, and in control.

Step One: Quick Reminder

The first time the behavior shows up, keep it light and quick. A simple question works best:

"Hey, are you giving your best effort right now? No? Could you? Yes? Great."

Sometimes even a short look, like a confused expression, can serve as a reminder. If the student already knows the standard, this subtle prompt may be all it takes to reset their behavior.

Step Two: Short Conversation

If the behavior continues, it's time for a direct but quick conversation. Choose one of your conversational approaches—Confused Look, Open-Ended Question, Closed-Ended Question, or I Need Your Help. The goal is to bring awareness and encourage the student to take ownership of their choices without dragging the whole class down.

Step Three: Sit Next to You

If the behavior still does not change, the student sits next to you. This is not a punishment but a pause for reflection. Call their name, point beside you, and say calmly:

"Sir, could you please sit next to me?"

If they ask why, don't get pulled into a debate. Simply repeat:

"I'm sorry, sir. Could you just please sit next to me right now?"

Once appropriately seated (on two knees or crisscross), allow them to sit in silence for 30–60 seconds. This gives the student space to reflect without distracting others.

When the time is right, have a short dialogue:

"Do you know why you're sitting next to me?"

If they don't, explain:

"I've had to remind you multiple times about your effort, so I thought it was best you sit here to think about it. If you want to return to class, you'll need to choose the correct behavior moving forward."

After another pause, ask:

"Are you ready to return to class?"

If they say yes, follow with:

"Are you going to choose the correct behavior for the rest of class?"

Once they commit, thank them and send them back.

Balance Is Key

The Three Address Rule only works if you stay balanced. If you remind them too many times, students stop taking you seriously. If you jump to sitting them out too quickly, you miss opportunities to teach responsibility. Each student is different, but the three steps give you a consistent framework.

Takeaways

- The Three Address Rule is a clear system that keeps corrections consistent, fair, and calm.

- Step One: Quick Reminder – Start light. Use a short question or a prompt to encourage self-correction.

- Step Two: Short Conversation – If behavior continues, use a Conversational Approach, such as the Confused Question, or I Need Your Help, to raise awareness and take responsibility.

- Step Three: Sit Next to You – If behavior still doesn't change, calmly ask the student to sit beside you to reflect—not as punishment, but as a pause for thinking.

- Always speak respectfully and keep your tone neutral; avoid frustration or sarcasm.

- Ask questions that make students think and encourage them to correct themselves.

- End every interaction with a respectful close and a clear commitment to correct behavior.

- The method only works if you stay balanced—too many reminders lose authority, but too much strictness kills connection.

- Consistency and calmness make this approach effective for both teaching and relationship-building.

PART 10

AGE & STAGE PLAYBOOKS

Every student is different, but patterns emerge when you look at age and stage of life. The way a 5-year-old learns is not the same as a 10-year-old, and neither is it the same as a teenager or adult. Each stage comes with its own motivations, challenges, and strengths.

Your role as the instructor is to understand these differences and adjust your approach. When you teach a young child the same way you teach an adult, frustration is almost guaranteed. But when you match your expectations, communication, and feedback to the stage of the student, you unlock progress.

This chapter is not about lowering standards. It's about setting them in the right way for each stage of development. Every age group is capable of focus, discipline, and growth, but how you help them reach those qualities will look different.

Think of this playbook as a set of lenses. Each lens helps you see your students more clearly so you can connect with them, catch the right moments, and coach them effectively. In the pages ahead, we'll walk through four key groups:

- **Ages 4–6:** Early learners who thrive on fun, repetition, and simple wins.

- **Ages 7–12:** Growing independence with a mix of peer approval and personal goals.

- **Ages 13–18:** Teenagers seeking identity, confidence, and respect.

- **Adults:** Mature learners motivated by progress, efficiency, and purpose.

By the end of this section, you'll not only know what to expect from each group—you'll know how to guide them with clarity and confidence.

AGES 3–6: BUILDING THE FOUNDATION

Children ages 4–6 are at one of the most formative stages of their lives. They are curious, full of energy, and eager to explore the world around them. At the same time, they are learning the basics of self-control, discipline, and focus. Your job as an instructor is not only to teach them skills but also to build the habits and attitudes that will support their growth for years to come.

At this age, attention spans are short, often only a few minutes at a time. They thrive on routine and repetition. The more predictable your structure, the more secure they feel. A class that feels scattered or inconsistent quickly loses them. The MENTOR Method works well here because it provides clear expectations, quick corrections, and lots of opportunities for praise.

What They Need Most

- Clear structure and routine.

- Frequent opportunities for success.

- Positive reinforcement is tied to effort, not just outcome.

- Simple, one-step instructions.

- Playful energy balanced with clear boundaries.

Common Challenges

- Short attention spans (they may drift quickly).

- High energy that can spill into silliness.

- Emotional reactions (crying, frustration, or sudden withdrawal).

- Difficulty separating from parents at times.

How to Engage Them

The key to success with this group is energy and connection. Use your presence to show that you are calm, confident, and fun to follow. Give clear, short directions—no more than one or two steps at a time. Use games and playful drills to disguise repetition. For example, instead of "do ten kicks," you might say, "kick the pad as fast as you can before I count to five."

Catch success early and often. A loud, cheerful "Yes!" paired with a high five can make a huge difference. This is also where body language matters most. So smile, bend down to eye level, and let them see that you enjoy being with them.

Discipline and Behavior

Discipline at this age should be quick, calm, and consistent. Long lectures or drawn-out conversations won't work—they simply don't have the attention span. Instead, use the Reminder Approach or quick redirection. If a student is goofing off in line, a lighthearted "Nope, eyes on me!" works better than a stern lecture. Keep it positive, keep it short, and move on.

Takeaways

- Ages 4–6 are all about building the foundation. Focus less on perfection, more on habits and attitudes.

- Keep structure simple and predictable; young children thrive on routine and repetition.

- Give short, clear directions—one or two steps at a time.

- Balance playful energy with clear boundaries; use games to disguise repetition.

- Praise effort, not just outcome, and celebrate small wins often.

- Keep corrections short and calm—use Reminder Approaches like the Confused Look or Cave Man Method.

- Avoid long talks; attention spans are short, and tone matters more than words.

- Maintain a warm presence by smiling, making eye contact, and engaging at their level.

- The more secure and connected they feel, the better they'll listen, learn, and grow.

Special Note on 3-Year-Olds

Some programs include students as young as three. While many of the same principles apply, you must lower your expectations and shorten your time frame even more.

At age three, children are still developing basic motor skills and emotional regulation. They may have trouble following group instructions, staying focused for more than a few minutes, or separating from parents. This is normal.

What to Adjust for 3-Year-Olds

- Keep activities short and be mindful of engagement.

- Focus on simple movements: standing tall, clapping, running to a spot, or balancing.

- Use exaggerated praise for effort, not outcome. Even trying deserves recognition.

- Allow for parental presence nearby if needed, gradually encouraging independence.

- End sessions with a quick win so the child leaves feeling successful.

Think of three-year-olds as "pre-foundation" students. You are not laying bricks yet—you are preparing the ground. Success at this age is measured by smiles, participation, and comfort in the group setting. If you can accomplish those, you've done your job.

AGES 7–12: BUILDING DISCIPLINE AND SKILL

Students ages 7–12 are entering the prime stage for developing discipline, skill, and resilience. Their focus and coordination are stronger than in early childhood, and they are capable of understanding more complex instructions. At the same time, they are highly influenced by peers and still motivated by praise from adults.

This age group thrives when expectations are clear and consistent. They want to know what success looks like and how to get there. They also want to feel that their effort matters, both to you and to their peers.

What They Need Most

- Clear rules and consistent follow-through.

- Opportunities to practice discipline and self-control.

- Balance between fun and seriousness.

- A sense of progress toward long-term goals.

- Recognition both in front of peers and in private.

Common Challenges

- Peer influence (students may misbehave if others do).
- Testing boundaries (they want to know if you mean what you say).
- Occasional resistance to effort (they may want to take the easy way out).
- Desire for fun that can compete with discipline.

How to Engage Them

Connection is still important, but this group also wants respect. They want to feel like you see them as capable, not just kids. Treat them with seriousness, but don't lose playfulness completely. Use challenges and competitions to keep them engaged—relay races, timed drills, or group challenges work well.

Your presence should be calm and confident, but also adaptable. Be firm when setting standards, but approachable enough that they feel comfortable asking questions. Students in this age group often respond best when they feel both supported and challenged.

Discipline and Behavior

Consistency is crucial. If you let one student get away with breaking the rules, the rest will notice. Always follow through. But balance correction with praise. For every time you confront a mistake, look for opportunities to reinforce when they meet expectations.

At this age, sarcasm or public embarrassment can do real damage. Keep corrections respectful and professional. Use short reminders, clear redirection, or a calm conversation when needed.

Takeaways

- Ages 7–12 are the discipline and skill-building years—students are ready for higher standards and clear expectations.

- Structure and consistency are essential; follow through on every rule.

- Balance fun with focus by using games, challenges, and competitions.

- Treat them with respect and seriousness so they feel capable and valued.

- Give specific praise tied to effort, both privately and publicly.

- Correct behavior calmly and respectfully; avoid sarcasm or embarrassment.

- Keep communication short, clear, and direct to maintain focus and authority.

- Reinforce discipline through steady expectations and positive accountability.

- The goal is to guide students toward self-control, confidence, and steady effort in everything they do.

Special Note on Pre-Teens (Ages 11–12)

Pre-teens are beginning to shift toward independence. They are more aware of themselves, their peers, and how they compare to others. This means they are more sensitive to correction and can feel embarrassed more easily. At the same time, they crave responsibility and want to be trusted with more.

What to Adjust for Pre-Teens

- Give them leadership roles when possible—leading a warm-up, helping a younger student, or demonstrating.

- Offer private feedback when the correction might embarrass them in front of peers.

- Encourage self-reflection by asking questions: "What did you notice about that kick?" rather than telling them directly.

- Begin tying skills to life lessons—responsibility, perseverance, and resilience.

- Keep expectations high, but make sure to show you believe they can meet them.

This stage prepares them for the teenage years. If you can help them see themselves as leaders-in-training, you give them a strong foundation for the challenges of adolescence.

AGES 13–18: DEVELOPING INDEPENDENCE AND RESILIENCE

Students ages 13–18 are in one of the most critical growth stages of their lives. They are forming identities, seeking independence, and learning how to navigate peer pressure, responsibility, and personal goals. At this stage, your role as instructor, coach, or teacher shifts. You are no longer just guiding—they expect to be treated with respect as emerging young adults.

This age group needs challenge and accountability, but delivered with respect and consistency. They will test limits not only to push boundaries but also to see if you truly care enough to hold them accountable.

What They Need Most

- Respect and to be treated as young adults, not children.

- Clear accountability without being talked down to.

- Opportunities to lead and take responsibility.

- Encouragement to persevere when things get hard.

- Mentorship that connects lessons to real-life challenges.

Common Challenges

- Resistance to authority occurs when they feel disrespected.

- Peer influence that can override your instruction.

- Fluctuating motivation—sometimes highly driven, other times disengaged.

- Heightened sensitivity to embarrassment or perceived unfairness.

How to Engage Them

The key with teenagers is respect. They can sense condescension instantly. If they feel you are talking down to them, they will tune you out. At the same time, don't swing too far the other way and treat them like peers—they still need you to be the authority.

Balance challenge and encouragement. Teenagers thrive on being pushed toward their limits, but they also need to know you are on their side. Share the "why" behind expectations—link discipline, resilience, and perseverance to the bigger picture of their future.

At this stage, leadership opportunities are powerful. Ask them to demonstrate, mentor younger students, or take on responsibilities. When they feel ownership, their engagement rises.

Discipline and Behavior

When addressing behavior with teens, the tone is everything. Stay calm, professional, and respectful. Never embarrass them in front of peers—this will backfire. Instead, use private conversations whenever possible. Ask guiding questions that help them reflect on themselves, rather than giving lectures.

For example, instead of saying:

"You're not paying attention."

Try:

"Do you feel like you're giving your best effort right now?"

This shifts the responsibility back to them without triggering defensiveness.

Takeaways

- Ages 13–18 are about developing independence and resilience. They want respect and responsibility.

- Treat them as young adults, not children; your tone should reflect equality and accountability.

- Provide clear standards and consistent follow-through; they will test limits to see if you truly care.

- Challenge them while showing genuine support because they respond best when they feel believed in.

- Use leadership roles and mentoring opportunities to build ownership and confidence.

- Explain the "why" behind rules and discipline to connect lessons to real-life growth.

- Address behavior privately and respectfully; public correction can damage trust.

- Ask reflective questions instead of lecturing to build self-awareness and responsibility.

- Balance authority with empathy. Firm, fair, and consistent guidance earns respect.

- The goal is to help them transition from dependence to self-driven, resilient young adults.

Special Note on Older Teens (Ages 16–18)

Older teens are on the edge of adulthood. They are making decisions about careers, education, and identity. At this age, your role as a mentor becomes even more important. They no longer just need correction—they need guidance for life.

What to Adjust for Older Teens

- Mentorship over management: Move from controlling to guiding. Treat them like partners in their growth.

- Life application: Tie lessons to real-world outcomes—discipline, resilience, and perseverance for work, relationships, and future goals.

- Respect first: Speak to them the way you would speak to a young adult, not a child.

- Ownership: Let them take more responsibility for their progress, even allowing them to fail and recover.

- Preparation for transition: Remind them that your role is to prepare them to stand on their own, not to always guide them step by step.

When older teens see you as a mentor who respects them and pushes them toward their future, they will give you their best effort—and often carry your lessons with them into adulthood.

ADULTS: RESPECT, RELEVANCE, AND RESULTS

Teaching adults is different from teaching children or teens. Adults come with more life experience, stronger opinions, and often a clearer sense of what they want. They are not in class because a parent signed them up—they are there by choice. Because of this, they need to feel that their time is respected and their goals are being met.

What sets adults apart is that they like to understand the *details* of what they're learning. They don't just want to copy a movement; they want to know *why* it works. They ask questions, look for logic, and appreciate when you take the time to explain how each part of a technique connects to power, balance, or control. When they understand the purpose behind what they're doing, they become far more engaged and motivated to improve.

What Adults Need Most

- Respect for their time and experience.

- Clear relevance—how this training connects to their goals.

- Practical feedback they can apply right away.

- Encouragement without being talked down to.

- A balance of challenge and support.

Common Challenges

- Adults can be sensitive to correction if it feels disrespectful.

- They may compare themselves to others and feel insecure.

- Time constraints from work, family, and responsibilities can make consistency difficult.

- Some are highly motivated, while others are casual participants.

How to Engage Them

With adults, engagement begins with respect. Speak to them as equals, not as children. This doesn't diminish your authority. It positions you as a steady, informed guide who genuinely values their effort.

Relevance is key. Adults want to know why they are doing something and how it benefits them. Link drills, lessons, or exercises directly to their goals, whether that's better health, stress relief, learning a skill, or personal growth.

Clarity matters too. Adults will disengage quickly if directions are unclear or if they feel their time is being wasted. Deliver instructions concisely, with enough detail to be useful but without over-explaining. When teaching technique, explain *why* each step matters—how a small adjustment in timing, posture, or angle creates a better result. This satisfies their curiosity and reinforces your credibility as an instructor.

Discipline and Behavior

Adults rarely act out the way children do, but they may disengage by checking out mentally, losing effort, or distracting others with side conversations. Handle these moments calmly and respectfully. A direct look, a question, or a reminder of the objective is usually enough.

When giving feedback, avoid a commanding tone. Instead, use a conversational style:

- Instead of: "You're doing that wrong."

- Try: "Could you rotate your wrist a little more here? That will make the technique stronger."

This approach keeps dignity intact while still guiding improvement.

Takeaways

- The adult student learns by choice, not obligation—respect their time and goals.

- Adults want to understand the details of the technique, not just copy movements.

- Connect every drill or lesson to real-life value and purpose.

- Speak as an equal while maintaining clear authority and professionalism.

- Give clear, detailed, but concise instructions to avoid over-explaining.

- Correct with respect using a calm, conversational tone.

- Handle disengagement with quiet confidence, not frustration.

- Adults stay motivated when they feel respected, informed, and improving.

- The goal is to create a learning environment built on respect, relevance, and results.

Special Note on Older Adults (Ages 50+)

Older adults bring unique strengths and challenges. Many seek training for health, mobility, or community rather than competition or mastery. They often carry years of discipline from careers or family life, but may also have physical limitations that require adjustments.

What to Adjust for Older Adults

- Safety first: Be mindful of joints, balance, and mobility. Modify drills when needed.

- Pace: Progress may be slower, but consistency matters more than speed.

- Respect experience: Acknowledge the wisdom they bring from life outside the classroom.

- Encouragement: Many older adults doubt their ability to improve physically. Celebrate even small wins to build confidence.

- Connection: For some, the social aspect is as important as the physical training. Building rapport helps them stay engaged.

Older adults thrive when instruction is encouraging, safe, and connected to long-term health and quality of life. When treated with respect and given achievable goals, they often become some of the most loyal and consistent students.

PART 11

SPECIAL CASES

SPECIAL CASES: WHEN THE USUAL APPROACH ISN'T ENOUGH

Most students fit into the broad patterns of age and stage. But every now and then, you'll meet a student who doesn't. Some are shy and barely speak. Others are bursting with so much energy they can't sit still. A few pick up skills unusually fast, while others struggle no matter how many times you explain.

These are the special cases. Instead of viewing them as problems, see them as openings for growth in your role as an instructor. Special cases stretch your patience, sharpen your skills, and prove whether you can truly apply the MENTOR Method to anyone.

The truth is, no two students are alike. Even within the same age group, personalities, abilities, and motivations vary widely. Your job is to recognize when the "usual" approach isn't working and adjust without lowering the standard. This doesn't mean changing your core values. It means finding the right path for the student to succeed while still holding them accountable.

In this section, we'll look at some of the most common special cases you'll encounter:

- **Shy and Introverted Students** – Building confidence step by step.

- **High-Energy or Distracted Students** – Channeling energy in the right direction.

- **Students with Learning Challenges** – Adapting expectations without lowering them.

- **Behavioral Challenges** – Confronting with clarity while keeping respect.

- **Gifted or Advanced Students** – Pushing them without skipping fundamentals.

- **Students Who Join Late or Transfer In** – Helping them catch up while protecting group flow.

Handled correctly, these students often become the most rewarding success stories. They remind us why teaching is about people first, skills second.

SHY AND INTROVERTED STUDENTS

Some students walk into the room ready to shout, move, and grab attention. Others enter quietly, avoiding eye contact and hoping not to be noticed. These are your shy or introverted students. They're fully capable, and what helps most is offering a path that brings out their confidence.

What They Need Most

- A sense of safety and security is required before they will engage.

- Clear structure so they know exactly what to expect.

- Small, achievable wins that build confidence.

- Encouragement that feels genuine, not forced.

- Time to warm up—rushing them often backfires.

Common Challenges

- Hesitant to speak loudly or respond with energy.

- Avoid eye contact and may physically withdraw.

- Take longer to engage with peers or group activities.

- May appear disinterested when in fact they are nervous.

How to Engage Them

Connection is your most powerful tool here. Start with small, one-on-one moments—learning their name, asking a simple question, or praising even the smallest effort. When they respond, celebrate it without making it a big public display. Too much spotlight too early can make them retreat further.

Use pair or small-group activities to ease them into participation. Place them next to a more confident peer so they have a model to follow. Keep instructions simple and give them a chance to watch others before trying.

Patience is key. Don't force loud responses right away. Instead, gradually raise the bar: first a whisper, then a quiet "yes, sir," then a louder one. Each step builds trust. Over time, most shy students begin to shine once they feel safe and supported.

Discipline and Behavior

Shy students rarely misbehave in obvious ways. Their challenge is more about a lack of response or disengagement. Handle this gently. A harsh confrontation may shut them down completely. Instead, use questions like:

- "Can you show me just one step?"

- "Can you give me your best try right now?"

These small requests keep them moving forward without overwhelming them.

Takeaways

- Shy and introverted students need safety before energy—they open up only after trust is built.

- Create a clear structure and predictable routines, so they know what to expect.

- Start with small wins and celebrate progress quietly but genuinely.

- Build confidence through private connection, not public pressure.

- Use pair or small-group drills to help them engage without feeling exposed.

- Give them time—confidence grows gradually, not instantly.

- Avoid forcing loud responses; increase energy in small, steady steps.

- When correcting, stay gentle and encouraging—never harsh or sarcastic.

- Ask for simple actions ("Can you show me one step?") to keep them moving forward.

- The goal is to help them feel safe, seen, and successful until their confidence begins to shine on its own.

HIGH-ENERGY OR DISTRACTED STUDENTS

Some students seem to have an endless battery. They bounce, talk, wiggle, and interrupt. While their energy can be frustrating, it's also a strength—if you know how to channel it. High-energy or easily distracted students aren't bad students; they simply need structure that turns their energy into focus.

What They Need Most

- Clear, consistent structure with no downtime.

- Frequent opportunities to move and stay active.

- Specific tasks to channel energy productively.

- Short, simple instructions that keep them on track.

- Positive reinforcement when they direct their energy the right way.

Common Challenges

- Talking out of turn, fidgeting, or distracting others.

- Struggling to sit still or wait their turn.

- Losing focus when instructions are too long.

- Testing limits with silliness, especially in groups.

How to Engage Them

The key is redirection, not suppression. If you try to force stillness too early, you'll lose them. Instead, give them roles and responsibilities that use their energy. For example:

- Let them help demonstrate a drill.

- Have them count for the group in a loud voice.

- Give them a challenge, like "See how fast you can set up this line."

Break instructions into bite-sized pieces. Instead of a five-step explanation, give one step, let them do it, then add the next. Use clear signals such as eye contact, a hand motion, or even moving closer to pull their focus back without calling them out harshly.

Routine is essential. When they know exactly what comes next, they are less likely to get distracted. Keep transitions between drills tight and purposeful. If you leave gaps, they will fill them with silliness.

Discipline and Behavior

When behavior crosses the line, act quickly and calmly. Don't get drawn into a power struggle or lecture—it only gives more attention to the behavior. Use the Reminder Approach:

- A short "Nope, eyes on me."

- A gesture toward the right behavior.

- A quick reset without extra words.

Balance correction with praise. The moment they channel energy correctly, call it out: "Great focus—that's exactly how I want to see it." The more you notice the good, the easier it is for them to repeat it.

Takeaways

- High-energy or distracted students don't need less energy. They need structure to channel it.

- Keep lessons fast-paced and consistent, leaving no downtime or gaps between drills.

- Use movement-based tasks such as demonstrations, counting, or quick challenges to direct energy productively.

- Give short, step-by-step instructions instead of long explanations.

- Use simple nonverbal cues like eye contact, hand signals, or proximity to regain focus.

- Maintain predictable routines; knowing what comes next keeps them grounded.

- Correct quickly and calmly using Reminder Approaches, not lectures or power struggles.

- Balance every correction with specific praise for focused effort.

- Turn their energy into purpose. Redirection over suppression keeps them engaged and learning.

- The goal is to transform high energy into drive, discipline, and leadership potential.

DEFIANT OR RESISTANT STUDENTS

Every instructor eventually meets a student who resists correction, refuses to participate, or openly challenges authority. At first, this can feel frustrating. Personal, even. But resistance is often less about you and more about the student's inner world. Defiance usually hides insecurity, fear, or a desire for control. Your role is not to overpower them but to guide them back into trust and respect.

What They Need Most

- Calm, steady authority without anger or sarcasm.

- Clear boundaries that are enforced consistently.

- Opportunities to make choices and feel ownership.

- Respectful communication that preserves dignity.

- Small wins that rebuild confidence and buy-in.

Common Challenges

- Talking back or refusing to follow instructions.

- Shutting down and refusing to participate.

- Testing boundaries to see if you'll enforce rules.

- Influencing peers to copy their behavior.

How to Engage Them

Stay calm and professional. The biggest risk is responding to defiance with frustration, because that reaction tends to intensify the situation. Instead, lower your voice, slow your pace, and keep your body language neutral. This communicates strength without drama.

Use questions to redirect instead of commands. For example:

- Instead of: "Do it now."

- Try: "What should you be doing right now?"

This shifts responsibility back to the student and avoids a head-to-head clash.

Give them controlled choices. For instance:

- "Would you like to demonstrate first or second?"

- "Do you want to start with the right side or the left?"

Choices give the student a sense of control while keeping them within your structure.

Connection is key. Often, defiance comes from a lack of trust. Find ways to connect outside of correction—ask about their day, notice their effort, or show interest in something they care about. Once trust is built, resistance often softens.

Discipline and Behavior

Defiant behavior must be addressed quickly, but never with humiliation. Avoid public arguments. If possible, use private conversations where you can lower defenses and speak respectfully.

Use the Three Address Rule:

1. First address: A quick reminder.

2. Second address: A short, calm conversation.

3. Third address: Have them sit out briefly to reflect, then invite them back when they're ready.

Always end corrections with a path back into the group. Leaving a student isolated too long turns defiance into resentment. The goal is restoration, not punishment.

Takeaways

- Defiance often hides fear, insecurity, or a need for control. It's rarely personal.

- Stay calm, steady, and respectful. Never match attitude with attitude.

- Maintain clear, consistent boundaries that are enforced without anger or sarcasm.

- Use questions instead of commands to shift responsibility back to the student.

- Offer controlled choices to give them a sense of ownership within the structure.

- Build connection and trust outside of correction. Find moments to show genuine care.

- Address resistance privately and calmly to avoid embarrassment or power struggles.

- Apply the Three Address Rule to correct behavior consistently and fairly.

- Always provide a clear way for the student to rejoin the group. Focus on restoration, not punishment.

- The goal is to turn resistance into respect and cooperation through calm authority and consistent care.

STUDENTS WITH LEARNING DIFFERENCES

Every student learns differently, but some face unique challenges such as ADHD, dyslexia, autism spectrum disorder, or other learning differences. These challenges do not define the student, but they do shape how they receive instruction, process information, and respond in class. As an instructor, your role goes beyond assigning labels. Your focus is on identifying the strategies that support their success.

What They Need Most

- Clear, consistent structure and predictable routines.

- Instructions broken into small, manageable steps.

- Patience and repetition without frustration from the instructor.

- Extra cues (visual, verbal, or physical) to reinforce learning.

- A safe, encouraging environment where mistakes are seen as part of learning.

Common Challenges

- Difficulty staying focused for long periods.

- Trouble processing verbal instructions without extra support.

- Sensitivity to noise, touch, or sudden changes.

- Slower progress compared to peers, which can cause frustration.

- Social struggles, such as difficulty working in pairs or groups.

How to Engage Them

Engagement begins with structure. Students with learning differences thrive on routines they can count on. Start class the same way each time so they feel secure. Give short, simple instructions and check for understanding before moving forward. When possible, pair verbal instruction with a demonstration or visual cue.

Patience is critical. Never compare their progress to others in front of the group. Instead, highlight their effort and consistency. For example, instead of saying, "You still don't have it," say, "I see you're trying harder each time. Let's keep building."

For students on the autism spectrum, transitions can be especially challenging. Prepare them by letting them know what's coming next instead of surprising them. For students with ADHD, use variety: change pace, add movement, and include hands-on drills that let them release energy while still practicing the skill.

Discipline and Behavior

When addressing behavior, keep it calm, consistent, and respectful. Students with learning differences aren't always acting out intentionally. Often, they feel overwhelmed, overstimulated, or uncertain about what's expected. Instead of escalating, redirect. A visual cue, gentle touch on the shoulder (if appropriate), or a short reminder often works better than a lecture.

Work with parents when possible. They can give you insight into what strategies work best for their child. This partnership not only helps the student but also builds trust with the family.

Takeaways

- Students with learning differences need structure, predictability, and patience more than anything else.

- Break instructions into small, clear steps, checking for understanding before moving on.

- Use multiple verbal, visual, and physical cues to reinforce learning.

- Keep tone calm and encouraging; never show frustration or compare progress publicly.

- Highlight effort and persistence instead of speed or perfection.

- Prepare students for transitions and changes to prevent anxiety or overload.

- For ADHD, include movement and variety; for autism, keep routines consistent and give warnings before shifts.

- Handle discipline with calm redirection, not punishment or embarrassment.

- Partner with parents to learn what strategies help their child succeed.

- The goal is to create an environment where every student feels capable, supported, and valued—no matter how they learn.

STUDENTS WITH PHYSICAL LIMITATIONS OR INJURIES

Not every student comes into your class with the same physical ability. Some may have temporary injuries, while others may live with permanent limitations. Either way, your role as an instructor is to create an environment where they can succeed, stay safe, and feel valued.

What They Need Most

- Safety first—always adjust drills to protect joints, balance, or recovery.

- Encouragement that focuses on effort, not comparison.

- Creative modifications so they can still participate fully.

- Respectful treatment—never make them feel "less than" the rest of the group.

- Progress measured against their own ability, not someone else's.

Common Challenges

- Risk of re-injury if pushed too hard.

- Frustration from not being able to do what others can.

- Isolation if they are pulled out too often or separated from the group.

- Overprotectiveness from parents or even themselves.

How to Engage Them

Stay positive and flexible. Instead of saying, "You can't do this drill," say, "Here's another way to do it." For example, if a student with a knee injury cannot kick high, give them a low kick target or focus on strong hand techniques. If a student has limited mobility, adjust stances or allow them to work from a seated position.

Always praise the effort, not just the outcome. "Great job snapping that punch!" is much more meaningful than "At least you tried." Be careful with tone—students know the difference between encouragement and pity.

In group settings, avoid singling them out as "different." Let them blend into the flow of class by quietly giving modifications. If others notice, use it as a teaching moment: "Everyone has different strengths. What matters most is giving your best."

Discipline and Behavior

Don't lower expectations for respect, effort, or focus. Students with limitations still need discipline and accountability like everyone else. What you adjust is the physical demand—not the standard of attitude and respect. This communicates that you believe in them and expect the best from them.

Takeaways

- Always prioritize safety first—adapt drills to protect joints, balance, and recovery.

- Focus feedback on effort and attitude, not comparison or limitation.

- Use creative modifications so every student can participate meaningfully.

- Treat them with respect, not pity—encouragement should sound genuine, not sympathetic.

- Keep progress individualized—measure growth against their own ability, not others.

- Avoid isolating students; quietly modify within the group to maintain inclusion.

- Use moments of difference as lessons in empathy and effort for the whole class.

- Maintain high expectations for respect, focus, and discipline; only adjust the physical demand.

- Stay positive and flexible—show that there's always a way to participate and improve.

- The goal is to make every student, regardless of limitation, feel capable, safe, and valued in your class.

PART 12

PRACTICAL EXAMPLES

The MENTOR Method isn't limited to martial arts—or even to teaching children. To prove this, let's examine how one of history's greatest coaches used these exact principles without ever knowing they had a name. Coach John Wooden never called it the MENTOR Method, but when you watch how he taught, you'll see Measure, Establish, Notice, Test, Observe, and Remind in action. His success proves these principles are universal.

PRACTICAL EXAMPLES OF USING THE MENTOR METHOD

John Wooden: A Coaching Example

One of the best examples of the MENTOR Method in action is the legendary basketball coach John Wooden. Wooden didn't just win games; he built people. He believed success came from doing the little things right every day, and his teaching reflected the same steps you've learned in this method.

When his players joined the team, the very first expectation he set was how to put on their socks and shoes correctly. That might sound simple, but he knew a wrinkle in a sock could lead to a blister, and a blister could keep a player off the court. He measured and established that expectation before they ever picked up a basketball.

As practice went on, he noticed every detail—footwork, body posture, even how players tied their shoes. He gave praise for small improvements but also tested them by raising the standard. If a player succeeded several times in a row, he would step back and let them prove they could do it on their own.

Wooden also understood the power of silence. During drills, he often watched without saying a word, observing to see if his players had truly mastered the skill. If they failed, he didn't jump in too quickly. He let them struggle because he knew real learning comes from figuring things out under pressure.

And he never stopped giving reminders. Wooden was famous for repeating the same lessons hundreds of times. He didn't see reminders as nagging. He saw them as essential. Mastery wasn't about learning something once—it was about practicing it until it became second nature.

John Wooden's coaching shows that greatness doesn't come from flashy speeches or complicated systems. It comes from laying brick after brick, expectation after expectation, until the foundation is strong. That's the heart of the MENTOR Method.

While Wooden's arena was the basketball court, the MENTOR Method applies to any place where children are learning and growing.

The Classroom Example

The MENTOR Method can also be used in the traditional classroom. Let's say you are a substitute teacher for the day. As you walk in, you measure the energy and vibe of the room. The students are full of energy and seem ready to test your authority. Right away, you know the first thing you must do is establish your authority as the teacher, or it's going to be a long day.

You calmly ask the students to take a seat. Most obey slowly, but a few boys lag behind. One of them, James, sits on the floor. You walk over, ask his name, and then directly tell him to find his seat. He shrugs, but he complies. You quickly realize James is the leader of the boys who are dragging their feet.

At this point, you decide the first expectation needs to be set: when your hand is raised, every student has five seconds to be in their seat, sitting properly with hands on their desk and eyes on you. After explaining this clearly, you have the students walk around the classroom. You then raise your hand and notice how they respond. This first time, it takes them 32 seconds—and James is last.

You tell the class it took them 32 seconds and calmly have them try again. This time, you test the expectation by adding positive competition: "Who can be the first to find their seat?" A girl named Olivia responds right away, and you immediately praise her: "Olivia was first to find her seat! Excellent job being ready in less than five seconds!" The rest of the class begins to follow her example.

But James continues to resist. You confront him directly, asking if he understands the expectation. When he says yes, you have him prove it on his own. To your surprise, he responds quickly and nails it. By addressing him directly, you not only correct his behavior but also earn the class's respect. They now see that you are paying attention and mean what you say.

As you move through the day, you observe the students, watching how well they stick to this expectation as you layer in new ones. When a few start to slip, you remind them quickly with a look, a raised eyebrow, or a short question. This keeps the standard alive.

This simple routine sets the tone. Students are positioned to learn because they know exactly what's expected, and they know you'll hold them to it. That's the power of the MENTOR Method in a classroom setting.

The Soccer Field Example

The MENTOR Method also works on the soccer field. Let's say you're coaching a group of eight-year-olds. When practice begins, you measure the group by watching how they warm up. Some kids jog, others kick the ball around, and a few are distracted. Right away, you know the first step is to establish focus and order.

You blow the whistle and tell everyone to line up on the sideline. A few kids respond quickly, but others drag their feet. You decide the expectation will be that, when the whistle blows, every player has 5 seconds to sprint to the line, stand tall, and look at the coach. You test this right away. The first time it takes 18 seconds. You calmly point this out and repeat the drill.

This time, one player hustles and gets it right. You immediately notice and praise him: "Ethan was first! That's exactly how we line up—fast, ready, and focused." The other players follow. After two or three tries, they're down to five seconds.

Later in practice, you set another expectation: every pass must be made with the inside of the foot. You observe closely, praising the players who get it right and correcting those who don't. When one player repeatedly uses the toe, you stop and remind the group of the expectation. You even have that player demonstrate the inside-foot pass correctly before continuing.

By the end of practice, the players know exactly what you expect, and they're sharper, more focused, and more disciplined. The same method that builds respect in the classroom also builds strong habits on the field.

The Youth Group Example

The MENTOR Method also applies in a youth group or church setting. Imagine you're leading a group of middle school students during a small-group discussion. As they come in, you measure the energy. They're loud, joking around, and not paying attention.

You immediately establish the first expectation: when you raise your hand, the group has three seconds to quiet down, sit up, and listen. You explain it once, then you test it. The first attempt takes much longer, so you reset it and try again.

This time, one student, Sophia, responds right away. You point it out: "Sophia, great job being ready to listen." Slowly, others follow her lead. After a few more rounds, the whole group responds in three seconds.

Later, as the discussion goes on, you set another expectation: when one person speaks, everyone else listens without interrupting. You observe carefully and praise those who wait their turn. When someone blurts out, you gently stop and remind them of the rule. Soon, the group learns how to respect one another's voices.

By using the MENTOR Method, you create structure without losing connection. The students see that you care enough to set clear expectations and hold them to it. Over time, this builds both respect and engagement.

The Parenting Example

The MENTOR Method also works at home. Let's say you're a parent trying to get your child ready for school in the morning. At the start of the day, you assess your child's mood and energy. Maybe they're slow to get out of bed and dragging their feet. You realize the first step is to establish a clear expectation: when the alarm goes off, they have five minutes to be dressed and at the breakfast table.

The first morning, you test it. It takes 15 minutes. You calmly point this out and reset the expectation. The next morning, you remind them of the five-minute standard. This time, they make it in eight minutes. You praise the effort: "You were much faster today. Great job getting to the table without me asking twice."

As the week goes on, you notice progress and celebrate it. When they hit the five-minute goal, you point it out and let them know they've met the expectation. If they slip back, you gently correct and remind them of the standard.

Later, you layer in another expectation: brushing teeth before leaving the house. At first, you have to stop them and reset it when they forget. But after a few consistent days, you see them do it on their own. That's when you move them into the observe phase, watching for mastery and giving encouragement.

Over time, your child develops both the habit and the discipline. You didn't just get them to follow directions. You guided them in creating a routine that eases mornings for both of you.

These examples show that the MENTOR Method is not tied to one place or one type of student. Whether in the classroom, on the field, at church, or in your home, the same process builds respect, order, and growth.

CONCLUSION

As an instructor, your work is never finished. Skills fade, students grow, and challenges shift. What stays the same is your responsibility to guide, lead, and serve. Teaching is not about a single class, a single belt, or even a single year—it's about the long arc of growth in your students and yourself.

This conclusion brings everything together with four reminders for the journey ahead:

- **The Long Game** — True success is measured over years, not days. Impact takes patience and persistence.

- **Raising the Standard** — Never settle. Your students will rise to the level you expect, and the standard you hold becomes the culture you create.

- **Genuine Care is Everything** — Students respond not just to skill, but to instructors who genuinely care about them as individuals.

- **Overcoming Burnout** — To lead for the long run, you must also protect your own energy, passion, and joy.

These closing chapters are not about new techniques or methods. They are about the mindset that sustains every other part of the MENTOR Method. If you carry these truths with you, you won't just become a better instructor—you'll become the kind of leader people never forget.

THE LONG GAME

Every great instructor knows this truth: you're not just teaching for today. You're teaching for who your students will become years from now. The long game is about patience, persistence, and perspective.

1. See Beyond the Immediate

It's easy to get frustrated when a student isn't picking up the material. But step back—what matters most is not how fast they learn today but that they stay engaged long enough to learn tomorrow. Progress is a marathon, not a sprint.

2. Value Retention Over Perfection

Students who stay for years will always surpass those who quit early, even if the "quitter" looked more talented in the beginning. Your focus should be on keeping students engaged, encouraged, and progressing, not just on polishing technique.

3. Teach Habits, Not Just Skills

Kicks, forms, drills—these are vehicles for something bigger. What lasts is the habit of discipline, the habit of focus, the habit of pushing through when it's hard. That's what carries into school, work, and life.

4. Plant Seeds Daily

You may not see the fruit of your teaching right away. Sometimes it takes months—or years—for a lesson to click. That's okay. Stay faithful in planting seeds of discipline, respect, and resilience.

5. Patience Pays Off

When you feel the urge to rush, remind yourself: students aren't meant to master everything at once. Your job is to guide them one step at a time while keeping them motivated to return for the next step.

Takeaway

The long game is about shaping lives, not just teaching lessons. Keep students engaged, focus on habits that last, and trust that seeds planted today will grow tomorrow.

RAISING THE STANDARD

The culture of your classroom is defined by the standards you set. Students will always rise, or fall, to the level you expect and enforce. Raising the standard is not about being harsh. It's about believing your students are capable of more and proving it through your consistency.

1. Your Standard Becomes Their Normal

If you let sloppy behavior slide, it becomes normal. If you insist on sharp responses, sharp becomes normal. Students adapt to whatever you consistently reinforce.

2. Model What You Expect

Students don't just listen to your words—they copy your behavior. If you want them to show respect, you must model respect. If you want them to give full effort, you must show full effort. Your example is the loudest standard.

3. Start Small, Build Big

Don't overwhelm students with too many standards at once. Start with one: quick responses, standing tall, or making eye contact. Once that becomes normal, raise the bar again. Progress is built by stacking standards over time.

4. Follow Through Every Time

The quickest way to lose authority is inconsistency. If you say, "Line up fast," but ignore students who don't, your words lose power. Every time you set a standard, you must be willing to confront it when it isn't met.

5. High Standards Build Confidence

Students feel proud when they meet real expectations. When you raise the standard, you raise their belief in themselves. Don't rob them of that pride by settling for less.

Takeaway

Students don't simply meet your hopes. They respond to the standards you establish and maintain. Raise the standard, model it, and follow through consistently.

GENUINE CARE IS EVERYTHING

All the systems, strategies, and methods in the world mean nothing if your students don't feel that you care about them. Genuine care is the foundation of influence. Without it, correction feels cold, and praise feels fake. With it, both correction and praise become powerful.

1. Care Beyond the Mat

Your care must go deeper than whether a student gets the drill right. Ask about their school, their family, and their interests. Celebrate their wins outside of class. When students feel seen as people, they listen more as students.

2. Correction With Care

Correction isn't just about fixing a mistake—it's about believing the student is capable of more. When care is present, even firm corrections feel like encouragement. Without care, even soft words can feel like criticism.

3. Show Up With Energy

Students know when you're checked out. Even on tired days, show them you value their time by being present, alert, and engaged. Care shows in your body language and tone as much as your words.

4. Small Gestures Matter

Sometimes it's the little things, such as a smile, a high five, or remembering their name, that make the biggest difference. These gestures communicate, "You matter to me."

5. Care Fuels Retention

Students stay where they feel valued. Parents notice it too. When you genuinely care, families trust you, respect you, and remain committed to your program long-term.

Takeaway

Genuine care is the foundation of influence. When students feel you care about them as people, your praise inspires, your correction motivates, and your impact lasts.

OVERCOMING BURNOUT

As you grow as an instructor, there will be times when you feel burned out and unmotivated to teach. This is normal. It's part of the process of doing anything day in and day out. Even after over two decades of teaching, I've experienced many days when I didn't feel excited to step onto the mat. The goal isn't to eliminate burnout entirely. It's about managing it so you can remain engaged and effective over time.

1. Acknowledge the Reality

Burnout doesn't mean you're failing. It means you're human. The repetition of teaching class after class can wear on even the most passionate instructor. By recognizing this ahead of time, you can respond with strategies instead of letting it derail you.

2. Shift Your Focus to the Students Who Matter Most

When motivation is low, think about the one student who excites you—the All-Star who always gives full effort, or the shy student who is finally making progress. Focusing on their growth can give you the spark you need to bring energy to the whole class.

3. Turn Class Into a Learning Lab for Yourself

Instead of just teaching, use the class to practice a skill you want to improve as an instructor. Maybe it's your voice, your timing, or a new way to connect with students. This reframes the class as an opportunity for your growth as well as theirs.

4. Create Something New

Burnout often comes from monotony. Designing a new drill or game can reignite your excitement. The anticipation of testing it out on your students not only engages them but refreshes you.

5. Plan Ahead to Remove Mental Fog

A big source of stress is stepping into class without a clear plan. Take time before class to visualize your drills, transitions, and objectives. Clarity creates confidence, and confidence fuels motivation.

6. Elevate Others

When energy is low, shift the spotlight to your assistant or mentees. Training them to step up as leaders gives you a sense of purpose that goes beyond the class itself. Watching them grow is deeply motivating.

7. Take Care of Your Body and Mind

Burnout isn't just mental. It's often physical. Too much caffeine, poor sleep, or lack of exercise all make it worse. Instead:

- Get regular rest and limit caffeine so it doesn't hurt tomorrow's focus.

- Stretch and move outside of class to recharge.

- Take a moment to pray or be still before class to reset your perspective.

8. Remember the Mission

When motivation feels lowest, remind yourself of the bigger purpose. Our mission isn't just to run drills—it's to help students become the people they were created to be. Keeping this vision front and center can be the push you need to get through difficult days.

Takeaway

Burnout is normal, but it doesn't have to control you. With the right strategies, you can turn low-energy days into powerful moments of growth for both you and your students.

THE JOURNEY AHEAD

Thank you for making it to the end of this book. I truly appreciate the time you've spent learning a method of teaching and leading that may be very different from what you're used to. My hope is that you find lasting success with your students or team. Success that brings joy and fulfillment to both you and them.

Like anything worth learning, this won't happen overnight. It takes practice, patience, and repetition. At first, it might feel awkward or unnatural, but over time, it will become second nature.

I'll never forget one of our instructors who moved from Virginia to work with us. His background was built entirely on the Authoritative method. The first time he taught a class (just one student, actually), he made it five minutes before stopping, looking over at me, and throwing his hands up in surrender. This was someone with over ten years of experience. But everything felt new again. That's normal. In fact, it's part of the process.

Fast forward to today, and he's one of our most effective instructors— and now trains others in the MENTOR Method. His growth was fast because he made one key decision: to set aside what he thought he knew and fully commit to learning something better.

If you'd like to connect, you can reach me directly at ko@thekoma.com. Whether you're interested in joining our team, becoming a partner in our franchise program, or simply want to share your thoughts about this book, I'd love to hear from you.

If you would like additional resources, practical tools, and updates that support the MENTOR Method, visit **TheMENTORMethodBook.com**.

If this book helped you teach, lead, or parent more effectively, please consider leaving an honest review on Amazon. Reviews help others decide if this book is right for them. If you believe it deserves five stars, that support truly helps this message reach more people.

Thank you again for reading. Keep learning, keep leading, and keep growing. God bless.

www.ingramcontent.com/pod-product-compliance
Lightning Source LLC
Chambersburg PA
CBHW060422130626
46555CB00005B/2175